CW00766822

Roger Bannister   Athlete and Philosopher

ROGER BANNISTER

Athlete and Philosopher

Peter Whitfield

Wychwood Editions
MMXXIV

Wychwood Editions

Chipping Norton   Oxfordshire

Privately Printed

Copyright Peter Whitfield 2024

Website
peterwhitfieldbooks Art- Ideas-History

Produced by Kopyrite Printers   Chipping Norton

With thanks to the Bodleian Library Oxford
for access to the Roger Bannister Archive

Cover picture: Vancouver 1954

Frontispiece artwork Doug Johnson

Contents

PART ONE: THE FOUNDATIONS

Prologue   7

1. The Child is Father to the Man   10

2. Oxford   15

3. Helsinki and After   25

4. Unfinished Business   30

5. Vindication: Running into History   35

6. The Last Act   39

PART TWO: THE STRUCTURE COMPLETED

7. Wider Perspectives   45

8. Metamorphosis   49

9. The Betterment of Society   53

10. The Vocation to Medicine   62

11. The Olympic Problem   65

12. Pembroke and After   73

Postscript: the Legacy   78

Appendix: The Track is Yours   82

Photographic Section   85

Sources and Bibliography   168

Index   169

*The London Olympic Games of 1948 was an inspirational event
for Roger Bannister and thousands of other young British athletes. It
signalled a resurgence of enthusiasm for sport after the austere days of
the war, and without the Games it is conceivable that Roger would not
have made his deep commitment to running. And it was his relative
failure at one Olympic Games which impelled him on to the
unique glory which he later achieved as an athlete.*

PART ONE: THE FOUNDATIONS

Prologue

On 30 December 1954, the BBC journal *The Listener,* printed the Queen's Christmas Day broadcast, which was, as always, a skilful message of hope and encouragement to her people in a time of trouble and uncertainty at home and abroad, as all times invariably are. On the very same page there appeared another message, considerably longer and more philosophical, which had been broadcast as a radio talk. It too was a reflection on the state not merely of the nation but of the world itself. This piece, entitled "Racing with Time", was the work of a private individual, not a high-ranking politician, not a religious leader, military commander or economic supremo, but an athlete, a young man who happened to be a doctor, but who was better known for having recently broken a running record. Put in these terms, it sounds extraordinary that this article should have been chosen to complement an address to the nation from the Queen of England. But the extraordinary was something that had become closely woven into the life story of the writer, who was Roger Bannister, a man whose name had been flashed around the world on 6 May 1954, when, on the University running track in Oxford, he became the first man to run a mile in under four minutes.

The story of Roger Bannister's athletic triumph and the way it changed his life is deeply fascinating on many levels. First, it is his personal story of how he worked out a philosophy of life, which was not a philosophy of words alone or even ideas, but of action and commitment; it therefore justifies being called an existential philosophy, which he expressed through his running. Secondly, the story has a powerful social dimension: the process by which he was accepted, taken up and embraced by thousands, indeed millions of people, primarily of course in Britain, but also by those in many other countries around the world. And thirdly, it is the story of his life after this great athletic feat – achieved when he was just twenty-five years old – and how he transferred his energies into the practice of medicine; how he moved on from the health of the individual to develop ideas and practical plans to improve the health of society itself, through what he believed was the therapeutic power of sport.

Through the summer months of 1954, after the four-minute mile, no one could foresee all this: it would emerge gradually over the following half century. But what is remarkable is how easily Roger Bannister stepped into the role of world-wide celebrity, and how perfectly he symbolised all that was positive about sport, about Britain, about a historic achievement such as his, and the opportunity that it gave him to inspire other people. The media at that time – newspapers, radio, early television, and Pathé News in the cinemas – never ceased to show and report his running, not only the Oxford mile, but his other great triumphs in what became a miraculous year for him. He was immediately bombarded with invitations, offers and honours; everyone wanted to see him, to know him and work with him, and they were not disappointed. He was intelligent and articulate, but also modest and possessed of a relaxed sense of humour and natural charm. Of all the athletes who might have run the first four-minute mile (not a large number it's true) it's hard to imagine any who could have received such adulation with such natural grace, or who could have responded to requests for broadcast talks or written articles of a standard fit to follow the Queen's address to the nation.

He accepted his celebrity as giving him a platform to articulate his views on life and on the social problems of his age in post-war Britain; the article in **The Listener** was perhaps the first public expression of these views. He points to the uncertainty of growing up in the 1930s, then being subsequently being plunged into the chaos of war. He is full of foreboding about the atomic age, the age of militant communism and the new Cold War, threatening as they seemed to do the very foundations of freedom and civilisation. Faced with these threats, what could the ordinary individual do? How could we cope with the sense of impotence which they generated? How could we avoid disenchantment, apathy, or a flight into escapism via films and television? Roger's answer was that the individual had to resist these forces of chaos and dehumanisation, and preserve his own self-respect at all costs. We had to find a means of channelling our creative energies and communicating our ideals to others. The future lay with the children and young adults, in whom we must encourage values built on effort and integrity, and on a sense of adventure that is both physical and intellectual. In his running he had sought and found a way of tapping into the sense of joy and purpose which was inside him, and he wanted others to discover themselves through sport as he had.

This was the motivation, the mindset, which drew him onwards through an athletic career which began while he was still a schoolboy. Several years before the four-minute mile he had already become a very well-known figure on the track and in the press, winning national championships and major international races. He was big news when he failed to win a medal at the 1952 Olympic Games in Helsinki, where he had certainly been among the favourites for the 1500 metres gold medal. At that time the world record for the mile stood at 4:1.4 to the Swedish runner Gunder Hägg, and speculation was rife about the possibility of breaking the four-minute barrier, with middle-distance runners around the world dreaming of becoming the one to seize that record.

When Roger became that man in May 1954, he was immediately elevated to the status of national, indeed international, hero. Those of us who lived through the 1950s will always remember the films and photographs of Roger hurling himself across the finish line and collapsing into the arms of friends and officials, like a man on the brink of death. In news terms he was suddenly numbered among figures such as Stirling Moss, Reg Harris, Dennis Compton and Stanley Matthews, all sportsmen who were accounted the best in the world, so that their names became household words. But even these comparisons do not do justice to Roger's fame and eminence, for there seemed to be something universal and historic in his achievement, that it was a triumph for mankind as a whole. Seeking for comparisons, the one that came most readily to mind was the first ascent of Mount Everest, almost exactly one year before, which was likewise seen as crossing a threshold of strength, courage and determination, so that the word "conquest" was applied to both. They were both seen as symbols of human progress, as asserting man's power to overcome the limitations which nature had imposed upon us. A parallel from America might be found in the first solo flight across the Atlantic in 1927, which made Charles Lindbergh's name famous throughout the world.

Roger's achievement was one of the events which seemed to define the decade of the fifties in Britain, which remains a fascinating period, appearing now to be poised on the edge of so much that was about to change. The early fifties in particular appears to be a time *before* everything that we now regard as modern: urban renewal and tower blocks; universal car ownership and motorways; the youth revolution and rock and roll; holidays abroad; sexual permissiveness; television; credit cards; angry young men; the media, which we used to call simply "the papers"; colour photographs and films to replace a world seen in black and white; electronic data was unknown, and homosexuality did not officially exist. This was a world without the rage for innovation that we now live with. And overshadowing the fifties was something almost too big to think about: the atom bomb, soon replaced by the hydrogen bomb, the symbol of human power to destroy everything, and which lent urgency and fear to the Cold War between Russia and the West, a conflict which might otherwise have been something that only politicians needed to worry about. Yet the fact is that the world destruction that was threatened never actually happened. What happened instead was a series of revolutions in society, in our thought, our way of life and our values, revolutions which merged into the world that we ourselves have remade, with consequences which look more and more like destruction. Throughout that process of deep change, Roger remained a link with the past, a symbol of continuity and positive values.

This book will give a narrative of the main events in Roger's career on the athletics track, and it will examine how the energy and the ideals which inspired his running were redirected into significant channels in medicine and sport administration. Far from remaining a symbol, a star or a figurehead, his later career was a constant process of work and renewal, of his dedication to the service of others, and to the ideals he had formed in his youth. It will try to analyse how first his running victories and then his ethical sense showed him how he might give practical form to his ideals in the fields of medicine, journalism and sports administration, reaching out to the nation as a whole.

Chapter One: THE CHILD IS FATHER TO THE MAN

Roger was born in March 1929 in Harrow, the London suburb that is home to the public school, famous as the school of, among others, Lord Byron and Winston Churchill. Anyone born in Harrow is asked about their connection with the school, but almost invariably there is none, as was the case with Roger, the only exception being that he used to do his training as a runner on the school cricket ground. His father, Ralph, was a civil servant who had moved to London from his native Lancashire, where his family had very deep roots, traceable to Robert de Banastre who proverbially "came over at the Norman Conquest". Roger wondered if he might have been one of the moustached figures portrayed on the Bayeux Tapestry; but he cautioned himself to bear in mind that, "Kind hearts are more than coronets, and simple faith than Norman blood." Nevertheless it remains true that through the centuries the Bannister name appears in many significant contexts in the history of Lancashire, including knights, landowners, Members of Parliament, and Mayors of towns like Preston. For some three centuries the family seat was Park Hill in Barrowford, now a National Heritage Centre south of Pendle Hill. Later members of the family went into farming, milling, wool, and finally the cotton industry. Roger's father, Ralph Bannister, was a young man of intelligence and ambition who made a deliberate decision to escape the hard and risky life in industrial Lancashire and move to a new life in London, where he married Alice, née Duckworth, also from Barrowford.

Roger's parents and upbringing were the primary shaping forces of his life and character. As a couple they were serious, well mannered, honest, hard-working, ethical, and largely self-educated. They believed that everything should be done properly, not shoddily or carelessly. They were not wealthy but they were independent, self-sufficient, and never in debt. Today we might think of them as puritanical, except that this word implies austerity and severity, but this was not true in their case. However, they were ambitious for their children, that they should receive the education which they themselves had missed, and anxious too that they should imbibe and understand positive values and live by them. They were not strongly religious however, and Roger's ideal of an ethic of service to humanity was apparently not inherited from them. At his junior schools Roger was one of those fortunate children who seemed to be good at everything. His school reports from the age of seven onwards, give him mostly A's, with nothing worse than B's. The reports summed him up as a well-behaved boy who enjoyed his school work and was eager to learn. His parents had every reason to be optimistic for his future.

His smooth path to that future was, however, interrupted by the air-raid sirens in September 1939. His family were rapidly removed to Bath, not as normal evacuees, but because his father's civil service department was moved there from Whitehall. The schools in Bath were filled with displaced London children, who were resented by their reluctant hosts, and a certain amount of warfare and bullying went on. Roger found himself on the receiving end, and as was the tradition in those days, he and the local boy involved were instructed to fight it out with the gloves on in the gym after school. Roger took considerable punishment from his tormentor before the fight was stopped, and this became a traumatic experience which he remembered for the rest of his life. He accepted that his fists would never be his real weapons in the battle of life, but that he would find other ways to strike back and maintain his self-respect. The story of this physical trauma is balanced by a psychological trauma also from his days at the school in Bath. He had inadvertently missed a rugby game in which his team had been badly defeated, and Roger was singled out by a vindictive master, and publicly labelled a rat. The experience of being punished for something done quite innocently is one that has happened to many children, and may be seen as one of the hazards of life in a school, or in any other community; to Roger it revealed the fragility of reputations, when success can so easily turn to failure.

In his second year he had already found an anchor in his young life, an ability which defused much of the stress of school, when he entered and won the school junior cross-country race over two and a half miles. He had already acquired the habit of running whenever possible, because, in his own words, "it was easier than walking." This race revealed something very important to him – that he could run and keep running when others could not, when they had given up in exhaustion. Moreover, there was an unexpected and highly practical sequel to this race, namely that he ceased to be bullied. Mysteriously, because he could run and win, he had become a kid who was OK, and he would be left in peace; he had found a new aspect to his identity. He went on to win this junior title for three successive years, and he recognised that his power as a runner was in some sense a natural gift, which he must nurture, and which might play an important part in his life. His personality and his interests began to mature, aided by his parents' gift of a bicycle, on which he explored the countryside around Bath, and even rode 100 miles to London alone in a single day. Once again his unusual natural strength was revealed, since very few children of fourteen would be up to such a challenge, physically or mentally. Roger never claimed any great success in technical or skill sports such as cricket, rugby, football or tennis, but it seems plausible to suggest that he could have succeeded in another endurance sport, cycling being the obvious one. His early victories in running, achieved with minimal training, remind us of the central fact that Roger was evidently a great natural athlete; he was winning from the start, and he kept on winning.

In 1944 the wartime evacuation ended and the family returned to London, even though the V-weapons were causing renewed destruction, but in 1942 Bath itself had suffered several nights of bombing in which 400 people were killed and hundreds of homes destroyed, so few places could really be called safe. This may have been in his parents' minds, for they were anxious for Roger's education to improve, and he had been offered a place in the hard-working but liberal independent University College School in Hampstead. Although aged only fifteen, he entered straight into the sixth form, and found it difficult to settle: he had lost the niche which he had made for himself in the Bath school, and was overawed by both staff and pupils. His self-confidence deserted him, and although his school work was always of a high standard he became driven in upon himself. There was no organised running at the school through which he might have asserted his personal strengths, and he became tense and nervous at home, not confiding his anxieties to his parents. Strangely perhaps it didn't occur to him to join a local running club, of which there were many in the London suburbs, and to run with them at weekends. He did a little rowing and a little rugby, but realised that he would never excel at either.

In desperation, he felt it was imperative to leave school at the end of the academic year, that is 1946. He had already decided that medicine was to be his life, that it would satisfy his intellectual demands and his humanist ideals, and he set about starting on the path to a medical career. He sat the Oxbridge entrance exams at age sixteen and did extraordinarily well, winning a scholarship which covered most of his costs, and his parents were only too delighted to give him their support too. Both Oxford and Cambridge offered him a place to study medicine, but Cambridge wished to defer it until the following year, while Oxford would take him immediately; thus his lifelong loyalty to Oxford had its origin in that random chance. This critical period at a new school had demonstrated important aspects of his character: that he had exceptional intelligence and capability, but that he was also sensitive, highly-strung and dependent on nervous energy, in a word that he lived an intense inner life, and when this got out of balance with the external world, he would suffer from anxiety and a sense of failure, which is always the downside for a person possessed of exceptional gifts. At Oxford he would leave behind much of the vulnerability of childhood, but not before he had recognised that he was in some sense a loner, and would remain so for a little longer. Although he set down this picture of himself as leaving school early to avert some crisis in his nervous personality, it is worth recording that his school reports show a picture of him at this time as brilliant in his work, motivated and co-operative, and an excellent house captain. They give no hint of his inner feelings, so whatever it was that troubled him, he concealed it very successfully.

How significant it is that the moment he arrived in Oxford and put down his suitcases in his rooms at Exeter College, he set off immediately to cross Magdalen Bridge to find the athletics track on Iffley Road, with the aim of re-igniting his neglected running career. For a time his passion for running had been dormant, but he always knew that running would play a vital role in his future life. When he came to write his autobiography, *First Four Minutes*, in 1955, he chose to begin the book with a childhood memory, a lyrical expression of the joy which he found in running:

What are the moments that stand out clearly when we look back on childhood and youth? I remember a moment when I stood barefoot on firm dry sand by the sea. The air had a special quality as if it had a life of its own. The sound of breakers on the shore shut out all others. I looked up at the clouds, like great white-sailed galleons, chasing proudly inland. I looked down at the regular ripples on the sand, and could not absorb so much beauty. I was taken aback – each of the myriad particles of sand was perfect in its way. I looked more closely, hoping perhaps that my eyes might detect some flaw. But for once there was nothing to detract from all this beauty. In this supreme moment I leapt in sheer joy. I was startled, and frightened, by the tremendous excitement that so few steps could create. I glanced around uneasily to see if anyone was watching. A few more steps – self-consciously now, and firmly gripping the original excitement. The earth seemed almost to move with me. I was running now, and a fresh rhythm entered my body. No longer conscious of my movements I discovered a new unity with nature. I had found a new source of power and beauty, a source I never dreamt existed. From intense moments like this, the love of running can grow.

Some readers have found this passage slightly exaggerated or pretentious for the autobiography of a sportsman, but I believe that this episode really happened, and to me it seems another childhood memory that he never forgot. Years later he would use this technique, this style, to make a serious attempt to go beyond a bare narrative of races and triumphs, and to capture the spirit of running as a life force; written in this spirit, his book became a genuine and significant self-portrait.

Chapter Two: OXFORD

Somebody told Roger that at Oxford a man without a sport is like a ship without a sail; here you could play as well as work, and the two would complement each other. Already, in 1945, his enthusiasm for running had been rekindled when his father took him to an international athletics meeting at London's White City stadium, the first such event since the war ended, which attracted a huge crowd of spectators. For Roger the chief interest lay in the 1500 metre race which featured Sydney Wooderson, the leading British middle-distance runner of the 1930s, who had held the world mile record in pre-war days. He was now matched against Arne Anderson, currently the second fastest miler in the world, and on paper far ahead of the Englishman. Not surprisingly, Wooderson was beaten, but the excitement of that day fired Roger's imagination, especially the enticing idea of the mile as the classic distance, the ideal balance between speed and stamina, and the race he longed to excel in. A few weeks after arriving in Oxford he finished second in the mile at the Freshmen's Sports with a time of 4:53 in this, his first competitive mile race. This was achieved on virtually no training, since his time was spent delighting in the freedom which he felt had opened up before him in the great world of Oxford, in which school became a distant memory.

The winter of 1946-47 was a severe one, and athletes' training was one minor casualty, which did not prevent the traditional Oxford versus Cambridge athletics meeting at the White City stadium in March of 1947. Roger was selected as a third string to run for Oxford in the mile. On a cold wet day, not knowing what to expect, he played a waiting game until the final lap, when, with nothing to lose, he exploded into the lead and won by twenty yards. He had felt that he had tapped into a hidden source of energy that was more psychological than physical, and he improved his time to 4 minutes 30 seconds. He was elated, sensing that he had now proved himself a true athlete, a feeling that was confirmed by a post-race party at which he met two great athletic figures from the past, Jack Lovelock and Harold Abrahams, both former Olympic champions. Lovelock, a New Zealander, was a graduate of Exeter College, who won the 1500 metres gold medal at the Berlin Games in 1936, and went on to become a doctor. Abrahams reached further back to Paris 1924 where he took the 100 metre gold, as dramatised in the film **Chariots of Fire.** Later that year Roger would bring his mile time down again, to 4 minutes 24 seconds; at the age of eighteen this held out the promise of his becoming an excellent miler in the next two or three years.

Not coming from one of the elite public schools or from a distinguished family, Roger felt no need to put on a show or play a flamboyant part at Oxford. He was happy to merge in with the background and to learn. At that time Oxford was full of ex-servicemen who were now undergraduates, and he found it humbling to be among men only a few years older than he was but who had been officers or driven tanks into battle or flown fighter planes. He must have been a quick learner, because at the end of his first year at Exeter he was awarded an endowed prize for the undergraduate "who has entered most fully and helpfully into the life of the college", and the prize was a very welcome cheque for £25. He was a member of a university athletics team which undertook a goodwill tour of German universities, where he was shaken to see the destruction wrought by British and American bombers. He found that winning races against men who had suffered such punishment and dreadful starvation brought him no satisfaction.

His thoughtfulness and modest demeanour impressed his fellow undergraduates and his elders, so that he was in demand for important administrative posts. He was elected president of the University Athletic Club and of the Junior Common Room of his college. Three years later he would become president of Vincent's, the elite Oxford sports club. In the first post he made a very full analysis of what he felt should be the way forward for the Athletics Club, and the main proposal was to lay a new running track to replace the quaint, uneven track that had existed beside the Iffley Road for as long as anyone could remember. This track was one third of a mile long and was raced clockwise, unlike every other track in England. This was pure tradition but it was given some kind of rationale, namely that it strengthened the left leg, and assuming that the right leg is stronger by nature, the result should be a perfectly even stride; this, it was claimed, was the secret of Oxford's undeniable success in turning out champion runners. Roger drew up an incredibly long and detailed plan of action to reform the Athletic Club in every conceivable way and wake it into new life.

I'm not sure if this plan was printed or widely circulated, but if it was the members must surely have thought that a thunderbolt had hit them. How much of it was translated into reality we have no way of knowing, but the new track was the biggest and most tangible feature of his plan, and the club was persuaded to back it. Incredible as it seems, Roger and the Club treasurer, another undergraduate, secured acceptance of the plan, and were given £50,000 to negotiate for the work with contractors; the new track was completed and inaugurated two years later.

From these formative years from 1946 to 1950, a fascinating diary survives, recording that he spent the six weeks before going to Oxford hill-walking in Derbyshire, presumably alone, with some light running in the open countryside. Then comes his very first race in Oxford, the mile in the Freshmen's Sports, mentioned above, where he writes "Took the lead from the start and beaten by T.P.E. Curry in final sprint, time 4:52. Sandy Duncan: "You can knock 20 seconds off if you stop bouncing." Readers of **First Four Minutes** may remember that passage, obviously transcribed verbatim from this diary in 1955. In 1949 he wrote, "Persuaded to run in University cross-country with almost no training. Won in fastest time for 22 years [41:54 for the 7½ miles] but terrific struggle with Gilbert in which I ran myself out up the Toast-Rack [hill] and somehow managed to sprint home." This is soon followed by, "Too much this season. I have been racing without training and the only reason why I have survived this is because of vast stores of nervous energy, which have been given time to recover after each race. But this is as bad as living on one's capital, and must cease." These passages show Roger to have been a most unusual young man: how many 17-year-olds would spend six weeks walking alone in Derbyshire? We wonder what was going through his mind as he pondered the fact that he was no longer a schoolboy, and would soon be a student at Oxford. Three years after his first race, he is winning without training one of the toughest races of the year. His belief in stores of nervous energy as his personal key to success was clearly formed already, and it was a conviction that he held to throughout his career.

In the midst of all this athletics-centred activity, Roger never forgot that the overriding goal of his life was to become a doctor, and this meant long hours of serious work in the lecture hall, the laboratory and the dissecting room. While still an undergraduate he had become drawn to the field of neurophysiology, the brain and the nervous system. The great Oxford figure, Sir Charles Sherrington, had pioneered physical research into the brain and nervous system, and hence the mind itself, for which he was awarded a Nobel Prize. To investigate this, the foundation of all that makes us human, seemed to Roger the highest possible goal of medical research. The other field which interested him deeply was respiratory physiology, the role of the lungs and the blood in carrying oxygen through the body, which is fundamental to life, and which plays a vital role in training for athletic activity. As a runner, this was obviously of more immediate practical interest to him than neurophysiology, and since a doctor's training was usually reckoned to be seven years he would have ample time to select the field in which he would finally specialise. His crucial medical exams at Oxford would come round in 1950, after which he would commence practical medical training in a series of hospitals. His first full-length medical study would be a thesis written as part of his B.Sc. on "Factors controlling respiration in severe exercise."

Roger had quickly become a notable figure in British athletics, perhaps through the combination of his attractive, and sometimes sensational, last lap victory bursts, and his position as president of the University Athletics Club. Nevertheless, late in 1947 he was surprised to be told that he was being considered for the British team which would contest the Olympic Games in London the following summer, even though at the time of the Games he would be only nineteen years of age. He declined the chance to run, but instead was happy to enlist as one of the hundreds of assistants who helped in their organisation, delivering messages between the senior staff and showing visitors around the Olympic sites. In the pre-Olympic months he won his second mile victory in the Oxford and Cambridge meeting, and won again in the Universities Athletic Union Championships. His first appearance in the national mile championship followed soon after, against by far the most serious competition that he had ever faced; he finished fifth but in a time of 4 minutes 17 seconds, his fastest mile to date.

The Games were widely seen as symbolising a new start, a re-awakening for Britain after the sacrifices and suffering of the war years. They have gone down in history as "The Austerity Games", which they certainly were, and by today's standards the final cost of £761,000 looks like a heroic exercise in economy. In athletic terms they were a great success, with huge crowds of 80,000 applauding the victors, most famously Holland's Fanny Blankers-Koen, who won three individual sprint golds, plus a fourth in the relay, and was enthusiastically acclaimed as "The Flying Housewife", which indeed she was. The Games were also the first international revelation of the great Zatopek in the long distance races, with a gold medal in the 10,000 metres, and a silver in the 5,000, missing his second gold by a fraction of a second. Britain had no gold medallists, but Tom Richards was a close second in the Marathon, while three different British women sprinters – Dorothy Manley, Audrey Williamson and Maureen Gardner – took the silvers behind Fanny B-K, with Gardner exactly equal with her on time in the sprint hurdles. The United States was dominant in the medals table, with Sweden in second place; Sweden had been neutral during the war so that their normal lives had been far less disrupted than Britain's. The 1500 metres race, the metric mile, was won by Erikssen of Sweden in 3 minutes 49.8 seconds, with two other Swedes finishing third and fifth. Of the three British entrants, only Bill Nankeville reached the final, in which he finished sixth; he would later win the national mile championship three times in succession; at this time championships were run by the A.A.A., the Amateur Athletic Association, known as "The Three A's". The 1500 metres was usually reckoned as around 18 seconds faster than the mile, so that Erikssen had a mile time equivalent to approximately 4 minutes 7 seconds. This was in a different league from Roger's best of 4 minutes 17 seconds, so we should probably conclude that he would have done outstandingly well to have reached the final, but that he would have had no realistic chance of a medal. He was wise to stay away, since a high intensity and high-profile defeat at his age might well have damaged his motivation and ended his career.

Not surprisingly the Germans and the Japanese were not admitted to the Games. But the great and the good who made the speeches opening and closing the Games spoke optimistically of, "This great common bond of sportsmanship that binds the youth of the world together," and of the time when the Games would be over, and those who had taken part in them had returned to their homes, "as torchbearers, with the flame of goodwill burning in their hearts, and continuing to burn there long after the Olympic flame has been extinguished." Roger was one of those who watched these races and heard these speeches, and they made a deep impression on him. He would later write:

The Olympic Games of 1948 changed my whole outlook. Until this time I had been inclined to look on athletics as a personal affair. I saw it primarily as a way of achieving that mastery over myself which I felt I was always in danger of losing – as I had done at school. I hoped my striving as an athlete would liberate other potentialities which I knew existed inside me. But when I was caught up in the Olympic movement … I grew outside my own feeble preoccupations and strivings on the track, and was transported to a greater realisation of the true significance of sport. Sport changed from being a jumbled striving of individual athletes and teams to a new unity, with a beauty that is evident in man's highest endeavour. In all this I felt proud to have a small part. Many of the principles that I had learned in Oxford I now discovered had existed for over two thousand years. The Greek ideal was that sport should be a preparation for life in general, the improvement of the whole man… When he revived the ancient Olympic Games in 1896, Baron Pierre de Coubertin was responsible for modifying the emphasis on individuality and victory – "The important thing is not the winning but the taking part. The essential thing in life is not conquering but fighting well." These were some of my thoughts as I watched the 1948 Olympic Games. I wondered in particular whether the Games were in danger of changing their nature. Was a new form of professionalism creeping in, with the athlete maintained by his country for the purposes of prestige? Might not the Olympic Games accentuate the political struggle between different nations? At the beginning of each Games such questions are raised. Then they are forgotten as the moving drama of success and failure unrolls itself.

Ideas like these are partly historical and partly intellectual, but they are woven together by a strongly emotional belief in the inspirational and therapeutic power of sport in general and running in particular; they are ideas which Roger would continue to develop, promoting them again and again in his published writings, in speeches and in lectures. On the strictly personal level, Roger learned from these Games that times which might win a mile race at a White City meeting were nothing like fast enough to win at this international level. He had been inspired by what he had seen, and was anxious to take his running up to a higher level. He was already thinking of the next Games in Helsinki, four years ahead, and saw his future as involving a steady intensification of his physical training and his mental concentration.

One of the fruits of Roger's presidency of the University Athletic Club was the revival of the international matches between an Oxford and Cambridge team and teams from the American Ivy League universities of Harvard, Yale, Cornell and

Princeton. These competitions had roots going back to the nineteenth century, and they had flourished in the inter-war years, but had naturally been in abeyance during the war until they were resumed in 1949. Roger was then twenty years of age, and his physique had developed in a way ideal for middle-distance running: over six feet tall, with long arms and legs and a powerful upper body, despite his practising no upper-body exercises. In the first match versus Cornell and Princeton he scored a clear victory over the Princeton captain in a time of 4 minutes 11 seconds, the second fastest mile in America to date in that season. A week later he again demonstrated his superiority against Harvard and Yale, in almost exactly the same time, which was his best ever. This prompted the distinguished coach and director of Harvard athletics, Bill Bingham, to state that Roger was the greatest miler he had ever seen.

Together with the other Oxbridge athletes, Roger was amazed at the sophisticated facilities and coaching structure of the American universities, while the Americans in their turn were taken aback by the performance of the British runners, whom they considered to be "uncoached." Roger's admiration for the American system was by no means uncritical, and he was concerned that the all-out drive for results threatened to turn the athletes into machines. At this time, and for most of his athletic career, he had no coach, feeling that he needed to be free to develop his running in his own way. Roger was known as an athlete whose training was light by the standards of other serious runners. For most of his mature career he would run 25 miles per week, but he had not yet reached quite that level. If he was under pressure with his studies, or the weather was very severe, he had no qualms about breaking training for several weeks at a time. He always enjoyed the winter cross-country season, which offered a relaxed, unfettered form of running which did not have to be taken too seriously, although he could and did win some hard-fought races over distances much longer than he ever ran on the track.

While in Princeton Roger had once more met Jack Lovelock, now a doctor in a New York hospital. Lovelock's health had deteriorated following a riding accident, when he was thrown by the horse. His eyesight had been affected and he suffered from dizzy spells. At the very end of 1949, Roger was shocked to learn that Lovelock had died, that he had fallen under a New York subway train. It was reported that he had fainted and fallen from the platform, but the cause was never absolutely proved, and the possibility of suicide could not be discounted. As a doctor, an Oxford graduate of

Roger Bannister   Athlete and Philosopher

Exeter College, an athlete, and a world mile record holder, Roger felt a great kinship with Lovelock, and he was deeply shocked by the manner of his death at the age of only thirty-nine.

For an undergraduate, Roger was able to squeeze in an extraordinary amount of athletics-based foreign travel. In 1949 and 1950 he visited Finland, Greece and Belgium, to compete either for Oxford or the A.A.A. He was already seeing these international competitions as invaluable experience in advance of the 1952 Olympic Games in Helsinki, for they had now become his all-consuming long-term goal. The longest of these foreign trips came at Christmas 1950 when he flew with a small team to New Zealand for the Centennial Games, which was a major international event. He won the mile convincingly, improving his time to 4 minutes 9.9 seconds, after which he set out to visit the school where Jack Lovelock spent his boyhood. Outside the school the oak sapling was growing that was given to the Olympic victors in Berlin. Once again he reflected on the sadness of a life cut short as Lovelock's had been, but also on the inspirational quality of his achievement for the athletes of New Zealand and for many others around the world, not least himself, an inspiration which would outlive the man himself.

In 1950 Roger successfully completed his exams for the first stage of his medical education. He was awarded a one-year research fellowship at Merton College, during which he resumed his earlier project of studying the physiology of respiration. He devised a motor-driven treadmill on which athletic guinea-pigs ran at various intensities while breathing different mixtures of gasses, and set about laboriously analysing the results. He was well aware that this research project was purely academic at this stage, and would not give him much practical help in his training, if any. It was very well known that to breathe a higher percentage of oxygen than normal can produce a sense of wellbeing and a rise in energy output. But since the gases that make up air are a more or less constant, this could be no help to the athlete, unless of course he were to run while breathing from an oxygen bottle. In fact it was around this time that bottled oxygen was being introduced for mountaineers when climbing at very high elevations such as the Himalayas. Roger was beginning to take an interest in mountaineering as an activity resembling the endurance sports, and he invited some mountaineers to be tested on the treadmill. He also conceived an interest in "somatyping", that is, classifying the different types of human physique as to height, weight and build, and suggesting athletic events which might be suitable for each one. He could not fail to notice with some satisfaction that his own physique – tall but not too tall, lightly built but not too lightly – was ideal for middle distance running. His interest in the physiology of running may seem slightly surprising, since he always believed and emphasised that the mental factors were decisive in realising one's full potential, and giving one runner the edge over another. But these experiments, although largely academic, probably helped Roger in some way, giving him a sense that he was analysing the barriers to faster running, and analysing how the boundaries of speed and endurance could be pushed back. His steadily growing fame led to the appearance of stories and photographs, and even television film, of Roger at work with his human guinea-pigs in his Oxford laboratory. These reports certainly gave the impression that he was using science to boost his strength, that he was a considerable jump ahead of his track rivals; this became part of the Bannister image as it was built up by the press, but the truth was somewhat more modest.

During these years, athletes in Britain and elsewhere were indeed pursuing new approaches to training, endeavouring to make it more systematic, if not fully scientific. It was instinctively understood already that the fundamental principle of training must be to push against resistance: in order to improve the body's strength, it was necessary to extend its effort up to and beyond the barriers of discomfort or even pain, before relaxing the effort. For a runner this meant repeated bursts of high activity, alternating with periods of recovery, which should be incomplete. A training session might include a series of quarter-miles run at a high effort, but not to exhaustion, interspersed by quarter miles at an easy pace. On a track this would translate into a lap on and a lap off, repeated perhaps five times, but steadily increasing to ten times. In this form it was called interval training, and it was an excellent way of building both strength and speed. Zatopek was the great exponent of interval training, but he took it to extremes, running at his height fifty laps or more, in sessions lasting well over two hours. Clearly track training of this kind could become monotonous, even soul-destroying, and an equivalent was introduced in more attractive surroundings. This seems to have originated in Sweden and was called *fartlek,* which means "speed-play." It was carried out in countryside, woodland or parkland, and consisted of a long, continuous, steady run, with random intervals taken at a higher speed. It was freer, more relaxed and instinctive than track intervals. Of course it demanded access to the right environment, but it was gentler on the legs than pounding the track or the road. It became known in Britain in the late forties and early fifties, and Roger was among the many middle and long-distance runners who adopted it. By 1951 he was running four or five times per week in sessions of five miles or more, considerably harder than he had trained before. He noticed that "speed-play" was well named, for it corresponded exactly to the way that children play: running around energetically until they are tired, then flopping down to rest, then getting up again in search of more action.

Early in 1951 he accepted the chance to go to America again to take part in a major athletics meeting in Philadelphia, where he would run in the Benjamin Franklin Mile, a prestigious invitation-only race. In April, two weeks before flying out, he ran a ¾ mile time-trial, paced for the first time in the early stages by Chris Chataway. This was not a racing distance, but an unofficial world record did stand to the Swede, Arne Andersson, of 2 minutes 56.6 seconds. Each of Roger's laps was faster than the one before, and his final time was 2:56.8, as close as it could possibly be without breaking Andersson's time. This distance appealed to Roger because it pointed the way towards the four-minute mile. "What would happen if I kept on running for another lap?" and "Could I have possibly kept on running?" These were the obvious questions that ran through his mind, but the answers were still out of reach when he left for America.

Roger had cleverly arranged to visit the University of Pennsylvania Medical School in order to study a new method of gas analysis which had not yet been tried in England. The mile race in which he was due to run was an elite event in the American athletics calendar. On arrival he was greeted by a reception party of pressmen eager to interview him, and they were astonished that he had travelled alone. One reporter summed up their view in the words, "No manager, no trainer, no masseur, no friends! He's nuts – or he's good!" The race would include two runners currently reckoned to be America's best milers, Fred Wilt and Dan Gehrman, both of whom had personal best times faster than Roger's. Before a crowd of 40,000 Roger ran steadily and within himself, following a runner whom he deduced was playing the role of pacemaker, while Wilt and Gehrman were behind him. Sensing that the two Americans were about to attack him, Roger took the lead just before the bell and set out alone to cover the last lap in 56 seconds, for a crushing victory and a new personal best time of 4 minutes 8 seconds – a time which he later discovered placed him in twentieth place on the all-time milers' list. It was a most impressive display of last-lap speed, which provoked the American journalists to wish that he would go back to England and stay there. Harold Abrahams commented, "What he needs now is confidence in his own ability. Modesty in Bannister amounts to an almost complete reluctance to acknowledge his greatness. He has the brains to plan and dominate the Olympic final as Lovelock did in 1936. To beat the world – and I believe he can – he must cultivate a purposeful aggression."

The highlight of the season would be the A.A.A. championships, and Roger was seen as the champion without a title, since in four or five years of serious specialisation in the mile he had never won the national championship. This time, in a race that was fast throughout, he could not produce an electrifying finish, but was still a clear winner in 4 minutes and 7 seconds, taking another second off his best time. At the age of twenty-two he was the national champion at last and was steadily improving his mile time. The goal of the Helsinki Olympics was looming larger and larger in his mind, but before the season ended his confidence received something of a jolt, when he read that the Swedish runner Landqvist, whom he had encountered before, had run 1500 metres in a time of 3 minutes 44.8, equivalent to a mile of 4 minutes and 3 seconds, which Roger knew was a great deal faster than he could hope to run at that moment. He had a winter's training and then two or three summer months in which to raise his speed to that new and higher level; it was the most serious challenge which he had yet faced.

Chapter Three: HELSINKI AND AFTER

Like the thousands of other runners who hoped to compete in Helsinki, Roger had to make a plan which would bring him to peak fitness in July 1952. In the autumn of 1951 he had begun his years of clinical training at St Mary's Hospital in Paddington, and his preparation had to fit in with working long hours and travelling to and from home. At St Mary's he came under the influence of the Dean, Charles, later Lord, Moran, well known as Churchill's doctor during the Second World War. Moran had founded a scholarship system enabling gifted sportsmen to study medicine, from which Roger benefited, although Moran's interest lay mainly in Rugby. Moran believed strongly in the character-building effects of sport, and wrote a famous book *The Anatomy of Courage* about his experiences in World War One, and the ability to come back from suffering and defeat and live a better life, a book which made a deep impression on Roger.

Roger felt very strongly that he was a nervous-energy runner who could produce only a few outstanding performances in one season. Linked to this, he inclined to be fearful of over-training, which he thought of as dragging the body down instead of building it up. Rest, he believed, was a vital ingredient of training, although many runners were reluctant to accept this. With these principles in mind, he determined on caution in his pre-Olympic training: he would not run cross-country this winter, nor commence any track-work until February at the earliest. Instead his training would be done on grass in the evenings, usually near his home in Harrow, on the school cricket ground. He would run in the free style of "speed-play" training, in sessions of around five miles, which were untimed. His plan was to bring himself to a peak by harbouring his physical and mental resources, rather than by subjecting himself to stress levels which he had never attempted before. He did not see this as a risky strategy because he believed that he knew himself better than any coaches or sports commentators did, however expert they might be.

Roger was now undoubtedly one of Britain's best-known athletes, and his progress towards the Olympic Games was a matter of national interest. Nevertheless he let it be known that he would not defend his A.A.A. mile championship in the summer, indeed he would not race at all over the mile distance. His plan was to race the half mile, to develop his already formidable speed over the shorter distance while conserving his basic strength. In fact he did run one mile at an inter-hospitals meeting, where he led from start to finish, in the moderate time of 4 minutes 10 seconds. He ran several speedy half-miles, and he won the national championship at that distance in the good but not brilliant time of 1:51, while Bill Nankeville took the mile victory in 4 minutes 9 seconds. Many people saw this as a race that Roger could and should have won, and public criticism of his plan became widespread. Why should Roger assume that he would be selected for the longer distance when he refused to race it as part of his preparation?

This criticism troubled him greatly, but he resisted the pressure to deflect him from his plan. Then just two weeks before the 1500 metre final he received a tremendous boost by running a ¾ mile time-trial, aided by Chris Chataway as a pace-maker. He recorded the almost unbelievable time of 2 minutes 52.9 seconds, which was nearly four seconds faster than the unofficial world record of 2 minutes 56.6 standing to Arne Andersson. He did not publicise this brilliant run, but for a short while he felt that his plan had been vindicated, and that he could go to Helsinki in his very best form, knowing that he had an excellent chance of winning the Olympic title.

The next day the newspapers published the detailed schedule of Olympic events, and he learned to his shock and disbelief that the organisers had added a third round to the 1500 meters competition: there would be a heat, a semi-final and then the final, making three races on three successive days. He knew at once that this was a disaster for him, that his training and his whole approach to racing had not prepared him for this. He felt betrayed by circumstances and by organisers who were not runners themselves and who apparently had no real understanding of what they had done - unless the reverse were true and it was sabotage. He asked Harold Abrahams to intervene on his behalf, but Abrahams said he could do nothing. This sudden change in the racing schedule had destroyed the possibility of proving that his approach to training had been right. He even wondered if he had been deliberately targeted by the officials. When he left to fly to Helsinki, his mood was unhappy and definitely pessimistic. It may not be an exaggeration to say that he was beaten before he started.

Roger shared a room with fellow Oxford athletes Chris Chataway and Nick Stacey, all sharing the same nervous apprehension and attempting to make light of it; sleep was difficult for all of them. Roger negotiated his 1500 metre heat in reasonable comfort, finishing third in a time equivalent to a mile of 4:13. The first of them to face a final was Chataway, who stayed close to the leaders, headed by the invincible Zatopek, through to the last lap when he launched his effort; but it was too soon and his rivals swept past him into the home straight, while Chataway stumbled and fell, finally taking fifth place, sixty yard behind Zatopek and the others. He later admitted that he fell out of sheer exhaustion, and could have played no part in the sprint. Roger was sick with disappointment, and his mood became still more fatalistic. His semi-final of the 1500 metres was won by the Belgian, Barthel, and was much faster than the heat, with the winner's time equating in mile terms to 4:8, only a hair's breadth slower than Roger's fastest time ever. At the finish he was drained, guessing that the final would be won in an even faster time, almost certainly beyond his capability. He later recalled the night before the final as one of the most unpleasant he had ever spent, sick with nervousness and self-doubt.

The final was contested by twelve runners, which Roger believed to be too many, leading to constant jostling and changes of position. He was content to run steadily in the middle, if only because he was too weary to do anything else. At the bell the runners were still bunched with no obvious sign who was the strongest. In the back straight Roger moved up onto the shoulder of the leader, and going into the last bend he was perfectly poised to surge forward as he had so often done in the past. But this time it was impossible: his body would not respond, he felt overcome with exhaustion, and could only watch as three runners in succession swept past him. He saw Barthel take the victory, with the American McMillen second on exactly the same time. The first five runners were covered by less than one second, and Roger was fourth, out of the medals. His immediate feeling was one of relief that the ordeal was over. Later he could take a justified pride in securing a time equivalent to a 4:4 mile, almost four seconds faster than he had ever run in his life. It was clear that he could have done no more, and he accepted the truth of the words of the Olympic motto, that taking part, fighting well, was the important thing.

Nevertheless he knew that the British public would be disappointed and the press vindictive, and in this he was right. The journalists called his performance out-right failure: "Roger wasn't nearly tough enough," wrote one, while another felt like "suing British athletes for breach of promise." The last comment was a reflection of the fact that the British team had returned from Helsinki without single individual gold medal, and with just one silver and three bronzes. Voices were raised in his defence, asking how coming fourth in an Olympic final in a time which had broken the existing Olympic record, could be called a failure. Yet Roger knew in his heart that failure it was. It was true that the change of schedule in the matter of the heats was beyond his control, but it was also true that this one adverse factor had thrown his entire plan into doubt and eventually to defeat. He had not been treated unfairly: all the runners had to face the same conditions and the same test. He and Chataway and the others could only marvel at Zatopek's unbelievable strength, winning three gold medals in a week in the longest events of all. Zatopek had trained for any conditions, he had prepared himself to the very limit of his power, so that if he were to be beaten it would have to be by someone genuinely and unarguably stronger than himself, no excuses or explanations would be accepted. Roger had never revealed the fabulous ¾ mile time-trial before the Games, which he saw as definitive proof that his training was producing the desired results, and he felt that to reveal it now would achieve nothing and only prolong the controversy.

In terms of sporting history the Helsinki Games saw the emergence of Russia as forming, with her East European satellites, a new sporting superpower overtopping even America's forty gold medals. British commentators asked if we would have to adopt a far more active stance towards sport in order to compete with them. The obvious answer was yes; but did we want our sports to go in that direction, and consign out traditional amateur ideals to history? Roger was keenly interested in this problem, and it played a part in the thoughts and plans which occupied his mind in the months after Helsinki. He has said many times that if he had won the gold medal at Helsinki, he would have stopped running and concentrated on his medical career. But now he decided that he could not do that, and his final decision was to continue, adopting as his new goals the British Empire Games and the European Championships which would take place in 1954. As he wrote later:

I wanted to prove that my attitude to training and running had been the right one, and hence restore my faith in myself that had been shaken by my Olympic defeat. I could accept being beaten in the Olympics – that had happened to many stronger favourites than me. What I objected to was that my defeat was taken by so many as proof that my way of training was wrong. I could not bear the thought that some other athlete might want to train along the lines that I had used, and that I might be held up as a bad example to dissuade him. My running had become something of a crusade. It was as if I were preaching a special attitude to running that I felt was right. It was a combination of the Greek approach I encountered at the Olympics, and of the University attitude that Oxford had taught me. I couple this with my own love of running as one of the most perfect forms of physical expression. I believed that many other potential athletes could experience this same satisfaction. If my attitude were right then it should be possible to achieve great success, and I wanted to see this happen, either for myself or my friends.

Chapter Four: **UNFINISHED BUSINESS**

So he was beginning again, with new goals, with something deeply important to prove, but also a very natural, very human desire to redeem himself. To do this however, he had to face the central fact that he had under-trained for Helsinki, that his creed of holding himself back and accumulating nervous energy, a creed which had served him so well in the past, had been in this case insufficient. The margin of that insufficiency was very small, it was tiny, it was less than a second, but it had been decisive, and in spite of his running faster than ever before, his finishing sprint had failed him. Therefore he must be prepared to re-think his approach to training, to demand from himself just that little extra effort and commitment. And after all why shouldn't he? He was still only twenty-three years old, and could therefore expect to be still gaining strength for at least two more years – two years in which to attend to this daunting piece of unfinished business. By a strange coincidence, as he was leaving Helsinki he met at the airport the highly regarded German coach, Woldemar Gerschler, who explained his method of adding quarter mile track intervals to the freer speed-play training, and since Gerschler was Barthel's coach, Roger had to listen. Roger learned that Barthel was a pure amateur, a working man, a chemist, who did all his training after work was over, just as Roger did, without any form of state support; this endeared him greatly to Roger.

A significant new factor during 1952 was that Roger had begun to form his triple alliance with the two Chrises, Brasher and Chataway, and together, even before Helsinki, the topic of the four-minute mile had been discussed between them. Chataway had led Roger for the first half of his ¾ mile record run, and Roger believed that this formula would be essential if the four-minute were to be achieved, indeed that it was a task for three men: two pacemakers and the fast-finisher. This was the training pattern which the three athletes would share over the next two years. Brasher was an experienced mountaineer, and the model they had in mind was the climb from a base camp to one or two intermediate camps, followed by the assault upon the summit. They had projected a possible attempt on the four-minute barrier after the Olympics and into the late summer, to mark the climax of Roger's career, after which he would retire from running. This plan was dropped after the events at Helsinki, and would later be seen to have been premature, since even Barthel had not closely approached the four-minute time. Roger would always give generous praise to the two Chrises, saying that his triumph had been a team effort, and this was not merely a conventional acknowledgement of help on one particular day, but a tribute to almost two years of companionship, mutual support and intense physical commitment on their part.

In the winter of 1952/3, Roger's training followed the same method as before, but at a slightly more intense level, and in the early spring he commenced track intervals, running up to ten quarter-miles at near-racing speed, with interval laps between. At this time he was attached to St Mary's Hospital and living in a room in Earl's Court, and he found it convenient to train in his lunch hour at Paddington track; because these sessions had to be brief, he made them as hard as he could, with virtually no warm-up. He also ran solo unpaced time-trials of half or three-quarters of a mile, the latter at fractionally outside three minutes. He was working a full day in the hospital, and was also trying hard to finish his Oxford physiology thesis, which was still hanging over him from two years before; it was finally published in a medical journal in 1954.

But even before the end of 1952, a completely new factor entered his planning, when news arrived from Australia that John Landy had run a mile in 4 minutes 2.1 seconds. This was the fastest mile anywhere in the world for seven years, and only weeks afterwards he achieved another mile of 4 minutes 2.6 seconds. Roger was astonished and disturbed: he could not relate these times to the Landy he had seen in Helsinki, and who had failed to reach the 1500 metres final. Speculation about the four-minute mile had been around for some years in athletic circles, but now there was no doubt that the race was on to be the first to hit that magic target. It was time to study the racing calendar and identify specific races where an attempt might be made using the three-man team which they had formed. The first opportunity was the Oxford versus the A.A.A. match in May at Iffley Road. When Roger's newly-built track had been opened four years earlier, he had promised himself that he would run his best races on it, and this was his chance. Chataway agreed to run at his fastest even pace for three laps, leaving Roger to finish alone. The result was not dramatic but definitely encouraging, the winning time being 4 minutes 3.6 seconds, a new British record and a four-second improvement on Roger's best time. It was a definite psychological boost, in that it was a time that would have won the Olympic race in Helsinki. The four-minute target was therefore not absolutely out of his reach, but to achieve it he had to improve just as much again: where was that improvement to come from? Meanwhile the American athlete, Wes Santee, hit the headlines with a mile of 4 minutes 2.4 seconds. Roger's nervous anticipation increased, for it seemed that at any moment he might open his newspaper and read that the four-minute mile had been achieved by Landy or Santee, or possibly by someone he had scarcely heard of. Had it not been for the fact that, in continental Europe, the mile is far less often run than the 1500 metres, he might also have worried about many of the runners who had been his rivals in Helsinki.

In mid-May he ran in an invitation three-quarter-mile race on Wimbledon track, which yielded the time of 2:59.8, but a gale-force wind was blowing and undoubtedly slowed him by several seconds. The next marker in his condition was a rather bizarre private time-trial that was squeezed into an inter-schools athletic meeting at London's Motspur Park track. Roger was paced for two laps by an Australian runner, Don MacMillan, after which Roger made contact with Chris Brasher, who had been ambling around the track waiting to be caught. Brasher then upped the speed but stayed just ahead of Roger to the finish, but without recording his own time. Roger's time was 4 minutes 2 seconds, on paper a further reduction of the British record. However the A.A.A. refused to ratify this time because it was not achieved in a genuine competitive race. Roger was not unduly surprised or upset, and it emerged that he had gone ahead with this trial only because he knew that on that very same day Wes Santee was making another attack on the four minutes and was predicting that he would do it. In fact Santee slowed from his previous time of 4:2 to 4:7. It would have been awkward and embarrassing if Roger had broken the four-minute barrier under those irregular circumstances, and he resolved that future attempts must be made in genuine competitive events. We may wonder why he did not target the A.A.A. championships in mid-July: would it not be splendid to break the four-minute barrier at the White City in the national championship? The answer seems to be that Roger made a clear distinction in his mind between a race which was a deliberate planned attempt at a record or a fast time, and a race in which winning was all-important – obviously true of a championship. Moreover he would certainly have realised that the A.A.A. would not welcome, or even tolerate, a three-man team parading in a championship.

This was Roger's last mile race of the season before turning his attention to his studies. But soon the season would be beginning in Australia, and he watched the sports news with great anxiety, expecting that Landy would immediately come out of his winter training with the sole aim of seizing the world record, if possible with the added glory of beating four minutes. Roger read all he could about Landy, who had come to the fore so soon after Helsinki, and who was reported to train far more intensively than he himself did. He had been formerly trained by Percy Cerutty, the charismatic and unconventional Australian coach, but at some point, not long after his disappointing result in Helsinki, he had split from Cerutty, and now devised his own training schedules. He had spoken with Zatopek and learned from him the merciless training regime which he followed, with the result that Landy now went in for sessions of up to twenty miles, totalling around 200 miles a month; and the results had started to come even before the end of 1952, when he ran 4:2 twice. It was a curious situation, but throughout the English winter of 53/54, while Roger concentrated on his own training, the image of John Landy, around the other side of the world, pounding the tracks of Australia in pursuit of the same prize as himself, was rarely far from his mind.

But during that time, Roger's own training was changing significantly, and the central feature of that change is that running for him was no longer a solitary activity: he was now sharing it with others, and in particular with two close running friends, Chris Brasher and Chris Chataway, one coaching expert, Franz Stampfl, and two journalists devoted to athletics, the famous twins, Ross and Norris McWhirter. Brasher and Chataway were themselves top-level athletes: Brasher would take the steeplechase gold medal in the 1956 Olympics, while Chataway would finish second to the great Russian, Vladimir Kuts, in the European Championships 5,000 metres in 1954. A few weeks after that race, Chataway became a national figure when he took his revenge against Kuts by defeating him at the White City and taking his world record as well. This race was broadcast live on BBC television, and it is said that a million viewers were on the edge of their seats as Chataway clung grimly to Kuts like a terrier, and in the final strides hurled himself across the line first.

Chataway was an Oxford man, Brasher a Cambridge man, and with Roger they were chiefly responsible for the concept of an Oxbridge school of running in the

Roger Bannister Athlete and Philosopher

1950s. Stampfl was an Austrian refugee who became first a school athletics coach, then set up as a private coach to a large number of athletes, and achieved a high degree of success. He was an educated, articulate teacher, capable of guiding and inspiring his pupils. Brasher and Chataway discovered Stampfl first, and they gently encouraged Roger to overcome his aversion to coaches, and in time Roger too was discussing his running with Stampfl, and accepting his help in planning his training schedules. It was Stampfl who kept them tightly focussed on the goal of mastering the quarter-mile intervals, ten of them, with the fast laps beginning with a base time of 65 seconds, and the aim of gradually bringing this down, nearer and nearer to 60 seconds, and even below. If this could be done, the athlete could convince himself that he might link four quarters together and achieve the magic time he was reaching for. It was a cease-less pushing and pushing against the resistance put up by the body and the mind, like hammering against a brick wall until it finally came tumbling down. I don't think that Roger officially enrolled with Stampfl, that Stampfl formally became his coach, fol-lowing many years when Roger had always said that he did not need a coach, that he didn't wish to become a running machine; but later he paid full tribute to Stampfl for his support in that crucial year. Roger was very struck by something that Stampfl once said: "The athlete defeats fear, and through it, conquers himself." This appealed to him in the light of his Helsinski experience. Brasher and Roger were regular training part-ners at the Paddington track in 1953 and 54, while Stampfl ran evening coaching ses-sions at Chelsea Barracks. The McWhirters were talented sprinters at Oxford, mov-ing later into newspaper journalism and sports commentary on television, so that their rather unusual names became virtually household words. They had their fingers on the pulse of athletics, they knew everyone, and they helped Roger in innumerable practical ways: timing his training sessions, driving him to meetings, and not least feeding him with the latest news in the international athletics world.

It was the McWhirters who reported John Landy's four-minute campaign during the English winter of 53/54. Every month a new race result would come in over the news agency wires, but none of them contained the words of a triumphant new world record. Through half a dozen attempts, Landy seemed stuck on 4:2 to 4:3, so that he had not yet equalled Gundar Haegg's world record of 4:1.4, which had been set nine years before, in 1945. But nor had Roger himself; in a sense he was relieved, but also mystified that Landy's massive recent training efforts seemed to be yielding no results. And he was worried, lest he should face the same brick wall: had middle-distance runners indeed reached the limits of what was possible? Who could say that Haegg's record would not stand for another nine years before a breakthough occurred? This was the background of mingled hope, uncertainty, excitement and tension in which the English athletic season of 1954 commenced.

Chapter Five: VINDICATION: RUNNING INTO HISTORY

December, January, February, March: athletes all over Britain, slow or fast, humble club runners or gold medal seekers, were grinding out their training miles through cold, wind, and rain, while winter turned into spring, the cross-country season ended, and their first track races were chosen. Among them the three Oxbridge flyers laid their plans in secret, like a group of commandos, planning their raid into the future, into a new era of athletic adventure.

As it happened the first possible race was the Oxford versus the A.A.A. at Iffley Road, exactly the same event in which, the previous year, Roger had slashed the British mile record to 4:3.6. During the winter those quarter-mile times had come down to 60 seconds, and had even nudged inside the one-minute, so they had the evidence they wanted. They had to train their minds to believe that the four-minute mile was achievable, that it was not an impenetrable barrier: it was just another time that happened to be a couple of seconds faster than Roger had run before. He had been training virtually every day for six months, building to his optimum strength, and now with less than one week to go, he paused his running and tried to think and act calmly, but in fact he was running the race over and over in his mind.

As Thursday 6 May dawned he realised immediately that there was a strong blustery wind blowing, and sensed at once that this was a bad omen, which must make the record far less likely. He took a noon train to Oxford, planning to spend a few calm hours with a friend. As he entered the train compartment, he was taken by surprise to find Franz Stampfl, and relieved to have someone so knowledgeable to talk to. Stampfl had obviously learned about the record attempt, although evidently not from Roger, and it seemed that a large number of other people had too. Someone, perhaps the McWhirters, had tipped off the BBC that it would be worth sending a camera crew to the Iffley Road track that day, and they accepted the advice. The two men talked about the weather problem, Roger knowing that he was at his peak but fearful that if he tried today and failed, he would have wasted vital energy and might be unable to make another worthwhile attempt for some time. Stampfl countered this argument by assuring Roger that he was confident that he was capable of running 3:56 or 3:57 under ideal conditions, and that therefore 3:59 was not out of reach even in that troublesome wind, which would after all help on one side of the track, as well as hindering on the other. He also argued that this might be his only chance for any number of reasons. If he let this chance slip by, and thereby lost the four-minute mile, he would never forgive himself. These arguments swayed Roger's mind, and he decided to leave a final decision until virtually the last moment before the late afternoon start, knowing that a blustery west wind will often begin to ease at that time. Warming up with Brasher and Chataway, they all felt that this was exactly what was happening: the wind was slackening just enough to make the record feasible; Roger signalled that the attempt was on.

Immediately after the gun they slipped into their pre-planned positions, Brasher leading, Roger behind him, and Chataway lying third, with, not surprisingly, the rest of the field soon distanced. Roger felt so full of nervous energy that he called to Brasher to go faster, but was ignored, Brasher knowing they were moving at exactly the target speed of 57.5 for the first lap. The half-mile was completed in 1:58, with Roger now feeling perfectly relaxed, having dismissed the wind from his thoughts. Chataway moved into the lead and gave everything to pull Roger to the bell in a fraction over 3 minutes. Roger must run the last lap in 59 seconds or less. As they came off the bend into the back straight Roger strode past Chataway and set out for home:

I felt that the moment of a lifetime had come. There was no pain, only a great unity of movement and aim. The world seemed to stand still, or did not exist. The only reality was the next two hundred yards of track under my feet. The tape meant finality – extinction perhaps. I felt at that moment that it was my chance to do one thing supremely well. I drove on, impelled by a combination of fear and pride. The air I breathed filled me with the spirit of the track where I had run my first race. The noise in my ears was that of the faithful Oxford crowd. Their hope and encouragement gave me greater strength. I had now turned the last bend and there were only fifty yards more. My body had long since exhausted all its energy, but it went on running just the same. The physical overdraft came only from greater willpower. This was the crucial moment when my legs were strong enough to carry me over the last few yards as they could never have done in previous years. With five yards to go to the tape, it seemed almost to recede. Would I ever reach it? ... I leapt at the tape like a man taking his last spring to save himself from the chasm that threatens to engulf him....I collapsed unconscious with an arm on either side of me... I knew that I had done it before I even heard the time. I was too close to have failed ... The stop-watches held the answer. The announcement of the result came – "Result of the one mile...time three minutes," and the rest was lost in the roar of excitement."

"The rest" was of course the words, "three minutes 59.4 seconds," verified by three independent stop-watches. That roar of excitement had only just begun, and over the coming weeks and months it would echo throughout Britain and much of the rest of the world. That very evening, the BBC was broadcasting the precious film they had made of every stride of the race. In the days immediately following, Roger had virtually to hide from the press, forced to escape from his parents' house in Harrow by climbing over back garden fences. In fact he retreated back to Oxford for a day, and needed a suitcase to hold all the letters and telegrams that were arriving, but he did not yet foresee that this was the beginning of a stream of fan-mail, invitations pro-posals and offers which would continue to flow for fifty years and more. Newspapers, radio and television could not get enough of the four-minute mile, it was a fairy story, and Roger was a wonderful prince: Oxford-educated, a young doctor, tall, well-spo-ken, smiling and almost handsome. It was also a British first, a world-class achieve-ment, paralleling that of the conquest of Everest in the previous year, so that what we now call the feel-good factor, but was then called euphoria, spread throughout the land like the spring sunshine. Strangest of all perhaps, the Foreign Office thought it would be a good idea to send him on a "goodwill visit" to America, which Roger agreed to, but which generated controversy and questions about possible payments and danger to his amateur status. Roger sailed smoothly through it all with dignity and humour as very few other athletes could have done, was scarcely off the air-waves for several days, and made a great impression; it was a sign of things to come. Soon after-wards he received offers from American sports companies to run as a professional, and be paid astronomical fees. One of these offers made him smile when he saw that the letter in question was addressed to "Roger Bannister, Oxford College, Cambridge, England," and he decided to remain an amateur.

If we ask why all this happened, why a young man running four times around a track for 239 seconds rather than 240 seconds, should excite millions of people around the world, the answer is wrapped in layers of speculation, uncertainty and even mystery; but perhaps it has to be sought in the mood of the time. Memories of the war were beginning to recede, and the austerity years of the 1940s were felt to be over at last. The Korean War had also ended, but that had been on the other side of the world. The venerable figure of Winston Churchill was back at the head of the government, and by contrast a young and beautiful queen was on the throne, inspiring thoughts of a new Elizabethan age. There was a willingness to take up new and exciting ideas and challenges which symbolised the best in the human spirit, this optimism feeding into a renewed faith in progress, whether those challenges were scientific, artistic, technological or humanitarian. In this atmosphere there was clearly a place for achievements that were more symbolic and inspirational than practical, and into this category came the first ascent of Everest, and undoubtedly the four-minute mile.

These achievements represented, if this isn't putting it too strongly, a break through into a new era, and, it's very important to add, an era which could see these things in films and photographs. They were, partly at least, products of the media age, of the entertainment industry, which played an enormous part in shaping the mood of the nation, in regenerating national pride. I am not suggesting for a moment that Roger Bannister, John Landy, Edmund Hilary or Sherpa Tensing set out to become stars; they did what they did out of a deep personal and private commitment. But they did in fact become stars, they "had greatness thrust upon them", because of the age in which they lived. All this is wisdom after the event, and perhaps it is stating no more than the obvious truth, that sport changes as the society around it changes. Because of the nature of the society in which he became a champion runner, Roger's life was changed forever; but changed only in certain superficial ways, for in others he remained faithful to his first and guiding ambition, namely to become a doctor, to master a scientific discipline and to use it to serve humanity. Roger knew of course that the press would be excited by the four-minute mile, but he was unprepared for the avalanche of publicity which followed the 6 May record. He had taken up running as an activity for a young man, but he knew there was more to him, than running; he looked forward to re-entering the real world and finding out what it would be.

Amidst all this discussion of achievement, adventure, heroism and stardom, a story is told – a story which was known to Roger – which may bring us back to reality and to a more philosophic view of sporting greatness. It relates that a philosophy class was in progress in the University of California, possibly in the year 1922, a class which was interrupted by the arrival of an excited student calling, "Sir, Sir, Nurmi has knocked two seconds off the world mile record!" The lecturer, who happened to be Chinese by birth, was equal to the occasion, and replied, "And how does the estimable Finnish gentleman intend to spend the valuable time that he has saved?" Whether this is pure invention or contains some core of truth, I really don't know.

Chapter Six: **THE LAST ACT**

Among the hundreds, or possibly thousands, of people who sent letters or telegrams of congratulation to Roger in May 1954, was John Landy. Naturally he paid tribute to his rival, but he must surely have felt bitterly disappointed that the prize which he had been chasing for a year and half had been snatched away from him. But far from being the end of Landy's connection with the world mile record, he was to play a decisive role in the next round of the great athletic events of 1954. Landy's telegram was sent not from Australia but from Finland, where he had set up in early May, in search of weather conditions and tracks which might yield better times than those at home. He won his first mile race in a time of 4 minutes 1.6 seconds, but did not improve on that. Chris Chataway, in a typically cavalier gesture, decided to go to Finland to challenge Landy, whose Achilles heel was thought to be his lack of a fast finish, and who Chataway thought he might defeat in an all-out sprint to the line. They met in Turku on 21 June and the result was sensational. After the first lap, Landy led in a fast even pace, until glancing behind him at the bell, he received a shock to see Chataway still on his heels. Landy took off and sped through the last lap alone, breaking the tape in 3 minutes 58 seconds, a new world record and the second breaking of the four-minute barrier. News of this race and the time stunned Roger: Landy's time was far beyond anything he had imagined possible. Roger had held the world record for just 46 days, he was doing very little training, and had lost much of his motivation. Now it was as if Landy had exploded a bomb underneath him, and he was no longer the world's fastest miler: he had been dethroned. Characteristically however, he sent Landy a telegram, congratulating him warmly, to which Landy replied that the conditions had been perfect, and he added, "I fancy it represents the absolute Landy limit," as if telling Roger what he would need to do to regain the record.

From a public point of view however, the Landy record was not bad news, it was sensational, for these two athletes, the only two milers in the world to have run under four minutes, were due to come face to face at the British Empire Games in Vancouver in just six weeks time; appropriately their meeting was already being dubbed "The Mile of the Century". Roger himself soon realised that the Oxford four-minute race was not the unsurpassable climax which he and everyone else had imagined it to be. Instead he now felt that he absolutely had to beat Landy. Why? Was it something to do with pride, honour, integrity, self-respect – old fashioned concepts like those? Yes, it must have been; but more generally it went back to Roger's crusade in defence of what he felt to be the classical or Oxford attitude to athletics, that he ran for the pure love of running, that his fame from the four-minute mile had brought honour and glory to that concept, but now it was once again threatened by Landy's victory and supremacy. Once again Roger had to vindicate his personal creed of running, otherwise he might be relegated to the position of a transitional record-holder, a first achiever who had quickly been overtaken and pushed aside because of his outdated ideals. The Vancouver mile now became a second challenge, as important as the first. But he realised that Landy was under essentially the same pressure: he had set a phenomenal new world record, but if he could not defeat Roger, he would be seen as second best, and his new record as an isolated gift from the gods of good fortune.

The pattern that the race would take must have been clear to the two runners long before they stepped onto the track. Landy was a pacer, a front runner who liked to lead and wear down his rivals. Bannister depended on his fabulous finish, his ability to turn on a last-lap burst of speed and sustain it for up to three hundred metres. This ability had given him so many victories, but had occasionally deserted him, most obviously in Helsinki. So it would be a clear and classic battle between the extended effort carried through four laps, and the last lap flash of speed, demoralising to the victim. In winning the A.A.A. mile championship for the last time just two weeks before flying out to Vancouver, Roger's time was a moderate 4 minutes 7 seconds, but his last lap was 53 seconds. This was an unmistakable message sent to Landy, telling him that he must run Roger off his legs with a fast pace if he were to have any chance of defeating him. Roger's task would be to fix his concentration on staying with Landy until the moment came, as late as possible, to strike past him.

After arriving in Vancouver, the days leading up to the big race were not encouraging for Roger. The two rivals met and chatted amicably, and Roger watched while Landy went through a track training session that was far more demanding than he himself would have undertaken at that stage. Landy too was using the quarter-mile intervals, and turned out ten, each one in 58 seconds, faster than Roger's and with a shorter interval. The effect on Roger was demoralising, and worse was to come, for a few days after settling in, he became aware that he had caught a cold, which proceeded to get worse and move into his chest. It seemed unthinkable to stop training, but he was forced to reduce its intensity quite drastically; it seemed he must rely on whatever speed he had already built up, he could not hope to acquire anything more. The days ticked by until the heats were run. Roger and Landy both qualified comfortably, Roger in 4 minutes 8 seconds, and the following day he was feeling distinctly better: a good sweat in the summer heat had obviously come just at the moment when it could cure the cold sufferer, rather than kill him. There would be eight runners in the final, but none except the two favourites was expected to play a serious part after the half-mile mark.

As expected Landy went into the lead almost immediately, for a first lap time of 58.2 seconds. Roger was more cautious on 59.2, and he let a small gap open up. This pattern was repeated in the second lap, so that by the half-mile mark Landy had a clear advantage of fifteen yards. It looked highly dangerous for Roger because he was now detached: effectively he also was a front runner with no help from Landy, no slipstream effect. It looked as if he might have made a tactical mistake in letting Landy get away like that in the hope that he would tire. Landy did not appear to gain any more after this point, but he was not slowing down either. Roger obviously saw the danger, and realised that he must close some of the gap at least in the third lap, before the bell, but he must do so without expending excessive energy. Fixing his eyes on Landy's figure ahead, he concentrated on pulling him back gradually yard by yard. This was the lap when milers usually tried to save a little strength for the finish, but in this case it was impossible to do that. At the bell for the last lap, Roger had succeeded in catching his man, and tucked himself in behind like a shadow. Along the back straight Landy seemed to increase his speed and Roger had difficulty holding him. He knew he must leave his sprint as late as possible because he was now approaching his limit. Together they pounded around the last bend, and Roger gathered himself to stride past Landy on the outside, and just as he did so he saw his rival glance momentarily behind him, on the inside. Roger realised that Landy did not know that he was directly behind him, perhaps because of the noise of the cheering crowd, and he realised too that this glance had given him an instant's advantage, that Landy was blind-sided. Roger leapt past him and hurled himself towards the tape, crossing the line five yards clear. His time was 3 minutes 58.8 seconds with Landy 0.8 seconds slower; they had both broken the four-minute barrier.

The crowd knew that they had witnessed a classic race, one that would be talked about for decades to come, an epic battle between two contrasting styles of running. They knew that Roger had risked defeat, not once but twice: by letting Landy go clear, and then by making an exhausting and unplanned effort to re-catch him. But he had also vindicated himself as a runner of unique gifts, who could tap into personal depths of courage and endurance to produce supreme performances which others could only marvel at. In Oxford, he had first demonstrated that he could run a carefully planned and controlled time-trial to reach a time unapproached by any other runner; and now in Vancouver he proved that he could win an intensely competitive race where plans were irrelevant. He would say many times that this was the most intense and memorable race of his life. It was followed by another famous race, but this time a tragic one, when the great British marathon runner, Jim Peters, entered the stadium with a clear lead but in the last stages of exhaustion, struggling but failing to reach the finish line, and being carried off the track semi-conscious.

Landy's world record would stand for a further three years, but he was destined never to win a major international competition. After Vancouver, he stopped running for six months, uncertain about his future. But in 1955 he came back and ran several four-minute miles, and felt he was strong enough to win at the Melbourne Olympics; but in a very close race he sadly had to accept the bronze medal. Wes Santee, who in June 1954 had run two miles in a single week with times of 4 minutes 0.7 seconds and 4 minutes 0.6 seconds, had then to enter military service and he ran no more for a year. When he did come back, he achieved a time 4 minutes 0.5 seconds, which remained his personal best, so unbelievably close to the magic four minutes, but kept apart by the unforgiving stop-watch. Another bizarre but amusing foot-note to the quest for the four-minute is worth recalling, centring on the great American runner, Mal Whitfield, who had been Olympic 800 metre champion twice, in London and in Helsinki, and who now fancied his chances of the big prize. He organised his attempt in a straight-out boardwalk race in Atlantic City in April 1954, which was wind-assisted and featured three pace-makers, including a British runner named Alec Breckenridge. The start was tremendously fast, so that Breckenridge was hanging on, and didn't get to the front until the half-way mark, when a new pacemak-er joined the field, completely against all the rules. Breckenridge felt strong and held the front with Whitfield on his heels, and that was the way they finished, with Whitfield four or five yards back. An announcement was soon made that Breckenridge had been disqualified because he was only a pace-maker. Whitfield's time was 4 minutes 6.9 seconds, and his version of events was that he had not tried to beat Breckenridge for the same reason – he was only a pace-maker! Breckenridge was urged to appeal, but the whole thing was so farcical that he refused to do so. He later moved up to marathon running, and represented the United States in the Rome Olympic marathon. This race, under conditions in which the record would never have been approved anyway, was a late and distinctly inglorious event in the great career of "Marvellous Mal."

After Vancouver, one more act remained in the drama of 1954, that miracu-lous year in Roger's life. The European Championships in Bern in August would be the setting for his last race, after which he would return to normal life and pursue his medical career. Before doing that he wanted very much to heal one wound that lay in his memory – his defeat in Helsinki. He wanted a second chance to somehow correct, wipe out, or redeem that defeat. It would be a similar kind of race between twelve men on a hot day in a European stadium with an unpredictable result, and he expect-ed that some of those men would be those he had run against in the Olympic race, including most notably the winner Barthel, and Lueg who had won the bronze ahead of Roger. Without being a certainty to win, he was certainly among the favourites but he was nervous before the heats, haunted by the fear of some mistake that would pre-vent him from qualifying for the final, leaving his career to end in a massive anticli-max after the glories of Iffley Road and Vancouver. In his heat he ran, in his own words, "Like a startled rabbit, darting up and down," and was relieved to finish third, safely into the final. To his astonishment he learned that Barthel had not qualified for the Luxembourg team, presumably an indication that his great form of 1952 had deserted him.

By the day of the final Roger had calmed down considerably. In contrast to Vancouver where he was in direct confrontation with a well-known opponent, he had made no plan for this race, content to let it unfold over the first three laps and stay out of trouble. In this he was wise, because after a false start the field bolted away from the line and there was an immediate collision, with one runner falling and having to abandon the race; Roger was forced to jump over him to avoid spiking him. After this unsettling episode, the pace soon slackened, and the half-mile was reached at well outside four-minute-mile speed. Through the bell Roger sat watchfully near the back of the field, then on the bend began to move up a few places, without making a decisive attack. Along the back straight he began to move past more runners, feeling strong, and instead of waiting, he determined to attack from the 220 metre mark, taking those in front by surprise. He took the lead on the bend running now at full speed, several yards clear as he entered the home straight. The field was strung out in a long line behind him, straining desperately, but powerless to catch him. Never had his finishing burst been better timed and never had it served him so well, for he was five or six yards clear on the line, at which for once he did not collapse, but looked coolly up at the clock to check his time.

It was 3 minutes 43.8 seconds, 1.4 seconds faster than Barthel's Olympic final: Roger could now feel that he had truly succeeded in laying the ghost of Helsinki. He had closed his career with three superb victories in three races. Berne, like Vancouver, had been an intensely competitive struggle, while the four-minute-mile had been a task of planning, concentration and mental control, driving his body single-mindedly to its limits. In each case he had stood up to the test and shown himself a complete runner. He had never claimed to be invincible on every occasion, but in 1954 he proved that in an important, targeted race, he was the best middle-distance runner in the world, worthy to take his place among the very best in the history of the sport. Never could Shakespeare's meditation on greatness have applied more aptly to anyone than to Roger: he had, it seems, been born great, with unique athletic gifts; he had used those gifts to achieve greatness; and he had still more greatness thrust upon him. All that remained now was to see what use he made of it away from the running track.

PART TWO: THE STRUCTURE COMPLETED

Chapter Seven: WIDER PERSPECTIVES

Aside from learning to cope with life as a world-wide celebrity, one more challenge faced Roger as 1954 moved into 1955. He wanted to tell his story, and he accepted the task as an opportunity to clarify his own thoughts about all that had happened, and to set down his philosophy of sport, its meaning for the life of the individual and for society generally. After Berne he took a six-week holiday, walking, hitch-hiking, and staying in youth hostels. It was during this holiday that he wrote the first draft of what became *First Four Minutes,* which was published in 1955 by Putnam.

This was and still is a remarkable work, one of the very few books to that date written by or about the life of a leading athlete. It was possible only because he happened to be highly literate, and had in fact always cherished the ambition to become a writer. To undertake it, Roger had to overcome his natural modesty and his reluctance to write about his own life and feelings. He succeeded in doing this by writing in a clear, precise narrative style, slightly distanced from everyday speech, always correct, smooth and flowing, but which is sometimes allowed to rise into evocative description, and occasionally into lyrical or dramatic passages interspersed among the factual content. I first read this book around the age of fifteen when I had begun to do a little running, and I dipped into it many time thereafter. I remember being fascinated by the epigraphs which stand at the head of each chapter, taken from poetry, works of fiction, the Bible and Shakespeare plays. I wondered how Roger had been clever enough to track down sixteen such quotations all mentioning running; only later did I learn there were such things as dictionaries of quotations. I was especially struck by the poem by Charles Sorley, a young poet killed in World War One, called "The Song of the Ungirt Runners", with it's final lines, "We run because we like it/ Through the broad bright land." I was also fascinated by the message which clearly lay at the heart of the whole book, that running was a means of expressing thoughts and feelings which apparently could not be expressed in any other way, and that running could become a vital part of a philosophy of life. Roger himself later sought to explain his motives in writing *First Four Minutes:*

Roger Bannister   Athlete and Philosopher

The book was written with both passion and purpose. The passion stemmed from having, after eight years of serious athletics, finally achieved my ambition to become the best miler in the world. It also arose from the nature of my running success, which had depended upon exerting my will-power and releasing nervous energy so as to push my body to its limits. At the age of twelve I found I had this gift of becoming very keyed up for the day of a big race and then, if required, driving myself beyond any bounds of normal physical strength. ...This special gift allowed me to succeed with less training than most of my contemporaries...Having become a true idealist about my running, my second purpose was to extol sport generally but running in particular, and then the Olympic movement, then substantially free from drugs and corruption. I wanted to portray running as a creative and self-fulfilling activity for youth around the world... to depict running, even when below an elite level, as a means of liberating young people from confusion and isolation, leading them instead to self-confidence and self-realisation.

These are recognisably the ideas which Roger would express in the *Listener* article discussed at the opening of this book. *First Four Minutes* was a highly successful book which sold in its thousands, and achieved its aim of inspiring many young runners to try harder in their sport, to enrich their lives. It was influential in leading other athletes, especially distance runners, to write their autobiographies, usually with the help of a ghost writer. Derek Ibbotson and Brian Hewson did this in the 1950s, followed by Gordon Pirie, and later Herb Elliott and Peter Snell. For me, fascinated as I was by the power of Herb Elliott's running, none of these other books came nearer to capturing my feelings about running than Roger's book did. There was also a special book about Zatopek, called *Zatopek the Marathon Victor*, published in Czechoslovakia, but in an English edition, which was also inspirational, although filled with communist propaganda to which I could not relate, but illustrated with wonderful photographs. Roger was stunned by Elliott's world record mile, and stunned again by his margin of victory at the Rome Olympics; but he detected that Elliott's hunger for running died after winning that gold medal, so that his career was over at the age of twenty-two. *First Four Minutes* was a farewell to Roger's running years, a statement of his sporting creed, and today it offers a marvellous evocation of its time. He donated half of his earnings from the book to the A.A.A. with which to build a running track in Harrow, which until then had no public track.

But he never did return to what other people regard as ordinary life, because wherever he went his name opened doors, and people wanted to know him and work with him. His running achievements had given him an immense platform from which to speak and to write whenever he wished. Yet, intriguingly, it was not just the runner that people wanted to know: the fact of his having run the first four-minute mile could not have smoothed his path to the distinguished career which he later enjoyed. Instead it was the man himself, his personality, his dignity and his good-humour which proved that is it not only what you do in life that is important, but how you do it. In **First Four Minutes,** he showed that he had both imagination and philosophical beliefs, and he portrayed running as an adventure, necessarily an adventure of youth. But our lives go in phases, and once the adventure of youth was over, it was time to move on to other phases, and he chose to dedicate his energy to medicine and to public service. It says a great deal about Bannister's character that he was able to walk away from his glittering athletic persona and address himself to a new life with entirely different goals.

Before leaving the running years, however, we must consider a subsidiary story that was evolving during Roger's career. In England in those years, athletics was popular sport which received a great deal of coverage in the sports news, and to anyone who followed athletics it became evident that there existed what we would now call a cultural division, if not an actual conflict, in British athletics. When Roger first arrived in Oxford, it could be said that Oxford and Cambridge together were the homes of amateur sport in the traditional sense: enthusiastic but gentlemanly, relaxed and insouciant. It was considered rather vulgar to train very hard for one's sport, and the conventional reason given was the obsessive fear of "going stale" and losing speed and freshness; the ideal was to triumph through natural, almost effortless superiority. Perhaps the classic expression of this philosophy came from Douglas Lowe, the Cambridge runner who won the 800 metre gold medal at both the 1924 and the 1928 Olympics, who remarked that, "Slight under-training is better than too much, that nauseates." Coaching certainly flourished, but much of it was directed towards style, educating runners in the correct movement of arms and legs, almost as if running were an aesthetic exercise, like ballet dancing. Roger was very different from the average runner: he was academic, intellectual, a trainee doctor who had his own ideas about the role of sport in a well-balanced life. The classical doctrine of **mens sana in** *corpore sano* – a healthy mind in a healthy body – expressed this principle. In other words he seemed to embody perfectly the Oxbridge approach to athletics. Now the press loved this image, and when Roger's name was coupled with the two Chrises, Chataway and Brasher, the identification was complete, and they became the three musketeers of Oxbridge running.

But there was an intriguing paradox waiting to emerge from this situation. The legendary achievement of the four-minute mile by those three, plus the defeat of Landy, seem to show that the Bannister vision of what running was had triumphed, since it was a gentleman amateur who had taken running into a new era. But in fact this was not so, for instead it was to be the relentless hard-work school of Zatopek, Landy, Kuts, and Herb Elliott that the future belonged. This was apparent even in England in the interesting figure of Gordon Pirie, who had run at Helsinki, and had finished fourth behind Zatopek in the 5,000 metre final, after Chataway fell. Pirie was a controversial character: brusque, pragmatic and opinionated, he was without a great deal of charm. But above all he was a fanatic about running, a real trier, who devoted endless hours to pounding the roads and tracks in search of a strength that no one else would be able match; he was deeply influence by Zatopek and coached by Gerschler. He was rewarded with more than one world record, and a victory over the famous Kuts in 1956, but he never won a gold medal at any major games. In the Melbourne Olympics in 1956 he was twice demolished by the almost inhuman power of Kuts – now suspected to have been fuelled by drugs. Pirie's prickly personality and his relative failure in international events made him a butt for the press, and he was repeatedly and very unjustly mocked by journalists.

Pirie made no secret of his scorn for the Oxbridge school, who, he claimed, wanted to win effortlessly. We could sum up his feelings by saying that Roger and the two Chrises were the Gentlemen, while he, Pirie, and other runners like Derek Ibbotson, Brian Hewson and Derek Johnson, were the Players. Pirie thought that Bannister could have run the mile in 3:56 in 1954 if he had trained harder, and that Chataway was a kind of playboy. He believed that the theory of aiming for a few peak performances per year was completely wrong, that a truly trained athlete should always be able to perform at the peak of condition. He claimed that the Oxbridge athletes were given special treatment by the authorities because they were Oxbridge men, in other words for reasons of class, and that Bannister's supposed use of science to help his running was a smokescreen to impress people. He saw the Oxbridge school as holding back British running, insulating it from what was happening in the world at large. Pirie was undoubtedly embittered by the criticism he had to endure, but in this respect he was a prophet of the future, in that world records and gold medals would indeed be won only by those who were prepared to devote themselves fanatically to the most intense training regimes. In spite of the great events of 1954, Pirie believed that the days of the Oxbridge school were over, perhaps indeed those events could be seen as the last fling of the gentleman-amateur. The potential enmity between Pirie and Bannister was defused later in the 1950s, when Pirie was suffering from an injury and losing form, and being subject to further rounds of severe criticism in the press. Roger was aware of this, and wrote to Pirie giving him his sympathy and support. Pirie was greatly touched by this act of kindness, and he never forgot it.

Landy's world mile record was trimmed by Derek Ibbotson in 1957, but less than a year later came the bombshell of Elliott's incredible 3:54.5 mile. This in turn was reduced by Peter Snell, and the athletics world was staggered when it learned the volume and intensity of the training of these two, who prepared like marathon runners. Snell in particular, under the guidance of his coach Arthur Lydiard, was clocking up 100 miles per week in basic strength training before commencing speed-work, and it transpired that Pirie's mileage was not far behind. This hard work school was directly inspired by Zatopek's example, seen as astonishing and revolutionary in its day, but soon to become commonplace. It would also become part of the process which saw the end of amateurism in athletics: training like this became impossible to integrate with a normal working life, so that for those determined to succeed at the highest level, professionalism was the only answer.

Chapter Eight: METAMORPHOSIS

Before Roger entered his new life, his miracle year had one more unique experience to offer him, namely falling in love and planning marriage. In fact it all began just weeks before the four-minute mile, at a party, when, in the words of the song, if it was not exactly "One enchanted evening," he certainly saw "a stranger across a crowded room, and flew to her side," and rather quickly "made her his own." Moyra

Jacobsson was an artist, the daughter of a distinguished Swedish economist and an English mother, who both lived in Switzerland. Her art work was skilled and attractive, and she planned a professional career as a painter, but marriage to Roger and raising a family of four children would mean a life so full and hectic that her art remained instead a private passion. Their marriage would take place in June 1955 in Basel, and afterwards they settled in West London, where Roger's medical career was largely spent. Here he would undergo the metamorphosis from athlete to doctor, to quasi-political activism, to neurological specialist; but through all these roles he would retain his unique position as a philosopher of sport.

Even before his marriage, the first great transition was to get used to being a full-time, qualified doctor attached to one hospital after another as his practical medical skills were honed. He might have done many other things, not least become a full-time author, for the quality of his writing was obvious. He might have written about sport and health, or popular science and medicine, about travel or current affairs – many forms of general non-fiction would have been open to him, and any publisher would have been eager to back his name. However, his dedication to medicine being absolute, he satisfied his writing urge and earned some extra money by going into journalism. *First Four Minutes* was serialised in the *Sunday Times,* which gave him the entrée into Fleet Street, and he accepted an offer from the same newspaper to become a roving athletics writer producing a dozen or more major articles a year; the paper could not conceivably have found a bigger name to add to their staff. In Oxford itself, the very select Achilles Club, open to Oxford and Cambridge athletes who had represented their university, had published an authoritative guide to athletics, and they swiftly recruited Roger to re-write the chapter on the mile in a new edition, to be published in 1955. Everything that Roger says in that chapter is correct and well expressed, but he is rather at a loss to explain briefly how to become a great runner, suggesting that in the end it all comes down to natural gifts and ability. He give no detailed advice on training, and holds to his creed: "I don't think it will ever be necessary for a miler to spend long hours running in order to get the most out of himself." The Oxford ideal was evidently still alive in Roger's heart, and he would never leave it entirely behind. In the notes that he made for that piece of work, he scribbled a few frank and self-revealing words about marathon running: "…Question whether it's worthwhile – like pole-squatting – must have a grudge against humanity…" It was not often that he made unguarded critical remarks like that about other athletes, but it's reassuring to know that he occasionally gave way to his feelings. Later, his views on marathon running would change completely.

His first appearance in **The Times** in August 1955 set the tone of all his journalism. Entitled "The Track is Yours" (see Appendix p.82) it set out Roger's philosophy of sport, especially running, as offering a pathway to freedom and self-discovery. "The Englishman plays games," he wrote, "with a fervour he seldom seems to devote to real life," and he sketches out Britain's enormous influence in the development of modern sport during the nineteenth century. He presents running as an escape from the deadening routine of everyday reality, as a return to an elemental activity that frees the mind as it strengthens the body. This was the creed which he would develop through much of his writing. He was especially concerned that this message should be taken to young people, boys and girls who felt unhappy, insecure or alienated from the adult world, and who needed to find motivation in their lives. To this end he committed his support to youth charities such as the National Association of Boys' Clubs, and the King George's Jubilee Trust (now merged with the Prince's Trust) while taking advantage of his *Sunday Times* platform to discuss these projects. He was particularly interested in encouraging sport and physical fitness as a route to helping deprived and problem children to find self-respect and meaning in their lives.

On the athletics front, he was sent to report on major events like the 1956 Melbourne Olympics and the 1958 Empire Games in Cardiff, a role he shared with the legendary Harold Abrahams. From Melbourne he described how the crowd was yearning for Landy to close his career with a gold medal, and how much he shared their hope. At the other extreme, he wrote in praise of cross-country running as the true heart of amateur athletics, writing with experience and great feeling about the camaraderie that athletes found in the rain and mud. Another subject that he referred to many times was the attempt to foresee the fastest speeds that athletes might possibly achieve in the future. He ventured a guess that 3 minutes 30 seconds could be the ultimate limit for the mile, but that it might take half a century to get there, and that the margin by which the record was improved would get narrower and narrower. This sounds logical, but in fact he was soon proved wrong, and he was staggered by the margin by which Herb Elliott broke the world record in 1958. Likewise his prediction in the 1950s of reaching 3:30 in fifty years now looks wildly optimistic: at this moment the world record stands to El Guerrouj with 3:43, set in 1999, so has the limit been reached? Later, while reporting on the Olympic Games in 1960, he was horrified by the heat in Rome in August, when traditionally everyone who could afford to do so left the city, and he wrote advising the athletes and others not to train because it could do them no good, but simply to rest. His recent army experiments with heat convinced him that distance runners in particular, would be in danger of collapsing in their events. Similarly he became particularly anxious about the Mexico Olympics of 1968, and warned about the possibility of athletes dying in the high altitude; this was a continuous theme of his journalism for two years or more.

He watched uneasily as the Olympics grew bigger and bigger, and increasingly involved in money and politics, because as the years passed it became clear that the gold-medal athlete had to become a professional. Should Britain therefore give state aid to Olympic athletes, he asked? And if we did not, was there any hope of breaking the American and Russian stranglehold on the Games? His instincts pulled him towards the "Sport For All" philosophy, rather than pouring money into sponsoring individual stars for the sake of national prestige. Meanwhile the increasing intensity of competition was leading athletes to turn to drugs, which he regarded as a complete betrayal of true sport.

It is clear from the pieces that he wrote that Roger realised that modern sport was becoming more complex, more commercial, more technical and more political than it had been when he was running. He regarded this with sadness, but saw it as an inevitable process, unfolding in obedience to the law that sport changes as the society around it changes. However he wrote other light-hearted pieces that revealed his sense of humour, even at his own expense; in one such piece he revealed that, among his fan-mail, he was regularly in receipt of marriage proposals, to which he scarcely knew how to reply, but that fortunately his wife, Moyra, took charge of those. He wrote many excellent book reviews, and significantly one of these was of the autobiography of his old sparring partner, Gordon Pirie, **Running Wild**, published in 1961. Roger's reading of the book was that Pirie was a man who had been soured by devoting himself to a harsh and fanatical training regime, which did not bring the results that he longed for. Roger felt his book should have concentrated on his achievements, which were considerable, and on the years which he was able to spend doing what he loved best, namely running. Pirie might be seen as one of sport's victims, in that he had sacrificed his life to it to the exclusion of everything else. His career looked like a reverse image of Roger's, for where running, despite all its stresses, brought Roger great freedom, self-fulfilment and a place at the heart of British athletics, for Pirie it brought enslavement to a punishing regime, a failure to achieve many victories at the highest level, and a position as a loner and a misfit. Pirie certainly did not deserve this reputation, and he might have achieved greater things had he not insisted in going his own way alone, and ended by becoming perhaps his own worst enemy.

Chapter Nine: THE BETTERMENT OF SOCIETY

Roger qualified as a doctor in 1954, and the professional testimonials that were written about him as he sought his first medical appointments all gave him an excellent character. In particular they mention the fact that he never allowed his great athletic achievements to interfere with his work. One of his former supervisors stated that his outstanding successes has left him, "completely unspoiled, and entirely free from any trace of personal conceit." In 1955, in reply to the many questions he was asked about his running plans, Roger issued a formal statement that he had retired completely from competitive running. However he did continue leisure running whenever he could, especially with his children. In fact the last race of his career came at a school sports day in 1965, when a "Fathers' Race" was organised. Since the distance was only eighty yards, Roger declined to enter, explaining that this was barely far enough for him even to get going. But the tragic disappointment on the face of his son compelled him to relent; so minus his jacket, but still with collar, tie and waistcoat, he gave it his best shot, and won by, as he said, "the thickness of his waistcoat button". This was positively his last appearance in competition.

Roger's involvement in youth work became more demanding and more high-profile in 1955 when he was invited to assist in setting up the Duke of Edinburgh Award scheme. Like the other charities which Roger worked with, the scheme aimed at enhancing the lives of young people by encouraging them to take up sport and adventure challenges requiring strength and endurance, often with an element of social or community service. These would be open-air activities to build physical fitness along with personal qualities such as self-reliance, initiative and care for others. The scheme was administered through schools, and the original architect behind it was Kurt Hahn, the Duke of Edinburgh's former headmaster at Gordonstoun, famous for his commitment to character building. Roger was struck by Hahn's well-known dictum that, "Sport is the moral equivalent of war," which he took to mean that sport could bring out qualities such as courage, endurance and self-sacrifice, just as war could. But he also conceded that it could have another, very different and negative meaning, closer to George Orwell's judgement that "Sport is war without the guns," which referred to bad-tempered, even violent games of football and rugby, where players can attack their opponents without actually killing them. Neither of these meanings seem to apply at all closely to athletics, but they give an idea of Hahn's brand of thinking. The psychologist, Anthony Storr, sided with Orwell when he defined sport as, "A ritualised, competitive struggle between members of the human species which does not result in slaughter." This definition clearly applies mostly to team sports, especially in front of massive crowds; it applies far less, if at all, to athletics. Among the other senior figures were Sir John Hunt, who had led the Everest expedition and Field Marshall Alexander, Rommel's nemesis in North Africa in World War Two. Medals would be awarded in different categories such as fitness, rescue, expedition, and service. This may give a rather rough, tough, boot-camp impression of military-style discipline for children, but nothing could be further from the truth, for the scheme was entirely voluntary, the motivation had to come from the participants themselves. Many thousands of award winners have explained how their lives were changed and their mental horizons transformed by their participation in the scheme. Roger was appointed as adviser to the scheme, in his dual role as a doctor and a champion athlete. The rationale behind his charity work was its essentially apolitical and personal nature: it was getting things done, through networks of like-minded people who had something important to offer to society, but had also an instinctive resistance to becoming entangled in the complex power structures of politics. He felt that the same approach motivated the other senior figures in the scheme too.

It seems strange to reflect that Roger's work for the improvement of society alongside elite, high-powered and royal figures, was interrupted by his call-up for National Service, and that he spent two years as an army doctor. Part of this time was in an army hospital in London, but for some six months he was posted to Aden, where a guerrilla war was in progress. Typically, Roger was not content to mark time and keep out of trouble, but instead embarked on an experimental study of the effects of intense heat on the soldiers, among whom there had been a number of deaths from heat exhaustion. He himself was among the guinea pigs who went through exercises in abnormal heat, and his findings led to changes in regulations, which took account of exposure to heat among army personnel around the world.

To Roger's work with children's charities, there was, so to speak, a literary aspect, which came in the form of a book, with the rather curious title of **Prospect,** sub-titled **The Schweppes Book of the New Generation,** bearing Roger's name on the title-page as "Advisory Editor". Sponsored by Schweppes – the background to this is not explained – this was an exercise in inspiration for young people, consisting of essays or self-portraits by young achievers in many fields: architecture, business, music, theatre, rock-climbing, service overseas, sport and so on. It would be easy to say that it seeks merely to spread "the sweet smell of success", but the time of its writing, 1961, (published 1962) suggests a more specific motive. Britain and much of the western world was then on the brink of the explosion of youth culture, often in its unattractive aspects: rock and roll, teddy-boys, mods and rockers, night-clubs, angry young men, flashy clothes, new-age films of rebellion, and so on. The message of the book seems to be that there's more to life than teenage games, and that everyone needs to find something serious to believe in. Roger makes this context clear when he says that we seem to talk about anti-heroes more than heroes these days. It is intriguing that no traditional careers are discussed – no army officers, no lawyers, no churchmen, nor even doctors; all these stories are of people who have invented their own identity. Two famous runners appear: Chris Chataway (but in his political capacity) and Herb Elliott. We might see it as an sociological survey in the form of personal anecdotes, but Roger adds weight to it when he quotes one of Burke's famous dictums: "Tell me what are the prevailing sentiments that occupy the minds of your young men, and I will tell you the character of the next generation," which sounds very well in theory, but is impossible to verify in practice. The book is an intriguing document, but it is more interesting for what it does not predict than for what it does.

Roger was not the only Bannister in demand for public service work, for between 1964 and 1974 Moyra too served on two high-profile committees of enquiry. The first was a Royal Commission to review primary education, known under the name of its chair, Lady Plowden. The work of the commission lasted for three years, and at the end its main recommendation was that children should attend nursery schools from the age of three. It also attracted huge publicity by urging that corporal punishment in schools should be abolished, which it was eventually, but not for a number of years. On the nursery schools for three-year olds, Moyra found herself disagreeing with all her colleagues. She believed that the scheme would be highly damaging to young children at the time when they stood in most need of their mothers' care and affection. Instead, she proposed a network of pre-school playgroups run by mothers themselves, with professional help and guidance. This idea formed the substance of the minority report which she submitted, in spite of attempts to dissuade her from doing so. In fact she would be proved to have been right, and the three-year-nurseries never materialised, while the playgroup movement went from strength to strength. Far from harming Moyra's reputation, this enhanced it, and in 1971 she found herself on the list to enquire into future policy on child health from birth to the age of eighteen. Once again she was out of step with the direction in which this enquiry was moving, in particular feeling that it was paying far too little attention to teenage problems, which had been very much in the news for the past decade. What the outcome of her dissent might have been is unknown, because injuries in a serious car accident (see below, page 64) persuaded her that she could not fight a battle of this kind at such a time, and she resigned.

Having said that Roger's motives in his voluntary social or administrative work were apolitical, his next step in that field was one of the most important in his post-athletic career, namely to accept a senior appointment on the newly-created Sports Council. He joined the Council in 1965 and would remain for nine years, initially as chairman of the research and statistics committee, and later as chairman of the Council itself. This major commitment sprang from his deep concern with the health and fitness of the nation's children, and a conviction that expenditure by the National Health Service of first millions then billions of pounds on curing people of their illnesses, should be balanced by social policies to avoid ill health that may have been preventable in the first place. Children's health in particular, had been previously neglected in public policy, and facilities for their sports would be top priorities. Those who had grown up in the 1940s and early 1950s would recall, with some irony, that the bombed sites which disfigured our big cities during the war, had actually opened up hundreds of adventure playgrounds for children to colonise, where they could run around and play to their heart's content; but these were lost in the wave of developments carried out in the 1950s in the name of slum clearance and urban renewal. The immediate post-war governments had had other priorities, but by the 1950s politicians began to see sport and health as linked policy areas, and to promote sport for genuine reasons of health, but also to gain plaudits from the electorate. A government enquiry was commissioned, chaired by Lord Wolfenden, which reported that an advisory sports council should be set up in order to produce a long-term plan for the provision of sports facilities for both children and adults. This report was published in 1960, and there was widespread excitement in the world of amateur sport as to who might be in line for a share in a ten million pound government hand-out.

The matter was far from cut and dried however, and it was not until 1964 when the new Labour government under Harold Wilson formally signalled that it would accept and act on this report, and in addition it would create the post of Minister of Sport, the first being Dennis Howell. This Sports Council would be an advisory body, to offer the government guidance on forming a strategic policy, and how money could be spent to achieve its policy aims. The Council would be in contact with the governing bodies of all major sports; it would direct large capital projects, most of them building sports centres, swimming pools, and other facilities; and it would carry out research and planning on a national scale, drawing up plans covering the whole of Britain. The long-term goal would be that the entire country should have access to decent sports facilities, in the form of indoor sports centres, swimming pools, open playing fields, and tracks for competition. The Council would draw up the spending budgets necessary to put these plans into practice; some of the money might come directly from the Treasury, but much of it would be channelled through local authorities. The initial budget was half a million pounds.

Since the war, it appeared that Britain had fallen behind other European countries in terms of success in Olympic Games and other international competition. Russia and the communist countries of Eastern Europe had identified sport as an area where national prestige and glory for the communist cause might be won, so they invested very heavily in it, and the Sports Council would have to spearhead Britain's response, which would be supported by millions of pounds of state funding. The political landscape in Britain changed very suddenly when the Conservatives won the 1969 general election, for they had been opposed to the establishment of the Council in the first place, and they felt generally that direct government involvement in sport was an undesirable extension of state power. They did not however abolish the Ministry of Sport, but came up with an alternative plan for a Sports Council that was executive and independent, like the Arts Council. This new, independent Council could state the national requirement for sport, under the slogan or banner of "Sport For All", and funds to realise their aims were raised significantly. Regional sports councils were set up to lobby and obtain finance for the facilities they wanted if they conformed to the general plans already made by the central Council. After a brief period of intense debate, the idea of the independent Council won the day, and the new Minister, Eldon Griffiths, asked Roger to become its chairman. Roger thought very carefully about the impact of this on his family and on his professional life, and decided that he must accept it, that this was his chance to do something historically important for British sport and for the nation's health. Just as on the day of the four-minute mile, when Franz Stampfl had asked him "What if this should turn out to be your only chance, and you rejected it, how would you forgive yourself later?" Roger now asked himself how could he turn his back on this opportunity?

The answer of course was that he could not, and the legislation creating the new independent Sports Council under royal charter was passed by Parliament, so that no politician in the future could decide to interfere with its work. A national plan for £120 million pounds of sports facilities – 1000 sports centres and 500 swimming pools – was published. Local authorities were eager to access this money and start work in pleasing their electorate with such popular schemes. Over the next fifty years British amateur sports were transformed as much as the health services had been. The governing bodies of numerous sports, some of them secretive power-structures run by a small coterie of men, were persuaded to reform themselves in return for Sport Council money. There were difficulties and conflicts, and the Sports Council had no legal power to force governing bodies into any particular action, provided it was legal. Strangely, Roger came into conflict with the A.A.A. which in the 1960s and 70s was being widely criticised by athletes for its autocratic rule over the sport, and as a consequence Roger fell out badly with the chairman, Harold Abrahams, who had been a lifelong friend.

In spite of this isolated incident, the balance sheet of the Council's performance was overwhelmingly successful, and much of the credit for that must go to Roger, to his prestige and the enormous goodwill that people felt towards him.

Politics once again intervened when the Conservative government fell in 1974 and Harold Wilson gave Dennis Howell his old job back as Minister of Sport. Howell had opposed the transition to the independent Sports Council, and had opposed many of its initiatives while he was in opposition. He could not breach its independence granted by the royal charter, but he could obviously make life far less pleasant for Roger than it had been. Knowing that the charter and his own legacy were now safe, Roger decided that this was the right moment to resign from the Council, after nine demanding but immensely rewarding years in the political maelstrom, and return exclusively to his role as a doctor and the head of a family. In his years at the council, he naturally learned a great deal about sports about which he had previously known little if anything, and he came to admire the immense variety of sports with which people found self-expression and enriched their lives. The one exception was boxing, which he grew more and more opposed to, especially in his capacity as a neurologist. Whenever the subject was raised, he would ask how a contest which consisted of attempts to inflict pain, injury and possibly severe brain damage on your opponent, could possibly be called a sport. However, as far as I know, he did not take active steps towards banning it, accepting that it was a matter of liberty and personal choice.

During his presidency, he had repeatedly urged the claim that sport had on the nation's financial support. "Sport," he argued, "is a natural, worthwhile and enjoyable form of human expression, and eminently deserves support in its own right and for its own sake. I would not like to imagine a world in which there were no games to play, no chance to satisfy the natural human instinct to run, to jump, to throw, to swim and to dance." He would point out that the Arts Council did not seek to justify the arts of music, painting, literature and drama, because they are their own justification, and sport comes into precisely the same category. This sounds convincing, but it is not a watertight case, for a purist might well reply that none of these things need be financed by the state, because they are natural, personal, creative activities which can and should be pursued by private individuals and their like-minded associates. The state need not intervene in the life of the musician, the poet, the painter or the runner, but leave these activities to flourish in the hands of enthusiasts. Indeed part of their attraction is precisely that these activities – or passions – exemplify the private life outside the control of the state.

From the national point of view, there was undoubtedly a feeling that British sportsmen and women were under-performing badly at the international level, so that an appetite existed for action to change this. It was as a reporter rather than a sports supremo that Roger attended the Munich Olympics in 1972, but the two roles came together in some of the entries which he made in his diary of the trip. These are brief jottings only, but they hint at important ideas: "People must get tired of [my] explaining why we are being left behind... Next step to accept that success depends on the level of government help – turn it into a machine." The last phrase is enigmatic, but it seems to suggest that at that time he was far from welcoming direct state subsidies for top athletes, and that his great focus was on the "Sport For All" principle, working from the grass roots upwards.

Roger's departure from the Sports Council was marked by a gathering of the great and the good in which the guest of honour was the Duke of Edinburgh, who presented Roger with a silver tray that was so heavy that he almost dropped it. He also received a knighthood, officially for his work for the Sports Council, but probably the opportunity was being taken to honour the man who, twenty-one years before, had run the first four-minute mile. In the same year however, he received a tribute of equal, but less visible value: he was given an award called the Sievert Prize, scarcely well known, but in the gift of the august body, "The Federation of Participants in the Olympic Games". This was an association dedicated to preserving the highest ideals of Olympic sport, as first set out by Baron Pierre de Coubertin, the founder of the modern Games. The award citation considered that Roger's athletic achievements had given enormous inspiration to young athletes around the world, and in addition to that, his subsequent work and his writings had articulated those ideals very powerfully. He played a great role in keeping alive the purity of amateur sport, and in encouraging philosophical thinking about sport. The citation quotes from Roger's own written statements concerning the value of athletics, going back to his journalism of 1955 (see Appendix, p...) but in particular to a speech which he gave in 1963 at an event marking the centenary of Pierre de Coubertin, founder of the modern Olympic Games. He begins by referring back to the childhood memory described in his book, *First Four Minutes.*

...I was startled and almost frightened by the tremendous excitement a few steps could create. It was an intense moment of discovery of a source of power and beauty that one had previously hardly dreamt existed. Now a scientist may attempt an

objective explanation of this … When we exercise, small electrical impulses pass all the time between our contracting muscles, our moving joints and our brains. The pattern of the electrical disturbance in the brain is presumably a source of pleasure because, like that caused by music, it has some interplay with the rhythms inherent in our own nervous systems…For an athlete the mystery of this simple situation always remains. He cannot explain it further, or if he could, he probably would not run well any more. He would not need to. ..What significance does sport have for the individual? I think adolescence can often be a time of conflict and bewilderment, and these years can be weathered more successfully if a boy develops some demanding activity that tests to the limit his body as well as his mind. Each adolescent has to find this activity for himself. It may be mountain-climbing, running or sailing, or it may be something quite differ-ent, it may not even be s sport at all. But by absorption in this pursuit, he forget him-self and it fills the void between the child and the man…We enjoy struggling to get the best out of ourselves, whether we play games of skill requiring quickness of eye and deftness of touch, or games of effort and endurance like athletics. There is a desire to find in sport a companionship with kindred people. Friendships which are formed under this baptism of fire have a curious permanence…As a result, sport leads to the most remarkable self-discovery, of limitations as well as abilities…These are my rea-sons for reiterating in a modern context Baron de Coubertin's views on the education-al necessity of sport, as he conceived it on a universal scale…Sport is a vital part of maturity too. For each of us it gives the chance to release a power that might otherwise remain locked away inside ourselves. I am sure that this urge to struggle lies latent in everyone, and the more restricted our lives become in other ways, the more necessary it will be to find some outlet for this craving for freedom.

I have quoted extensively from this speech because it sums up many of the ideas, the developing creed, which Roger first began working on during the writing of *First Four Minutes*, and stated again on many occasions throughout his life; it was this kind of writing that made Roger a pioneer in the philosophy of sport. In a final tribute to him, the Sievert citation picks out the opening paragraph from that book, describing a child discovering the joy and freedom of running on the seashore, and very cleverly links it with Isaac Newton's famous words:

I know not what I may seem to the world, but as to myself, I seem to have been only like a boy playing on the seashore and diverting myself in now and then finding a smoother pebble or a prettier shell than ordinary, whilst the great ocean of truth lay all undiscovered before me.

Roger would surely have been delighted by this comparison, with its faith that the child is father to the man; that in such delights as running on a seashore may lie the beginning of a life of mental freedom and wisdom; of discovering through play that man is most a man when he plays. Later, some years after leaving the Sports Council, he became seriously concerned at the growing practice of selling school playing fields and reducing the teaching of Physical Education in schools. He felt that this was betrayal of children, a negation of his creed of developing a balanced way of life, and that children were losing the habit of outdoor play and adventure, being left to fill their lives with television, and later, with electronic games.

Chapter Ten: THE VOCATION TO MEDICINE

In the midst of all this charity work and quasi-political work, Roger was always at heart a doctor and a medical researcher, because medicine was to him an objective way of serving humanity. His career was spent almost entirely in London hospitals, beginning immediately after qualifying in 1954 at St Mary's Paddington, with which he would enjoy a long association. A little later he found an additional post in the National Hospital in Queen Square, Bloomsbury, founded in the mid-Victorian age as the first specialist neurological hospital in the world, before even the celebrated Salpêtriè Hospital in Paris. Roger's memories, written and oral, of his days as a newly-qualified young doctor, take us back inside the health service as it was only seven or eight years after it was created, to life in a large teaching hospital before the age of ultra-sophisticated equipment and highly advanced drugs. Here the consultants were still the monarchs of all they surveyed, larger-than-life figures, very like the James Robertson Justice character, Sir Lancelot Spratt, in the classic film **Doctor in the House**, released in 1954. It's tempting to imagine that Roger's early experiences resembled those of the medical students in that film, played by Dirk Bogarde, Donald Sinden and Kenneth Moore. Rather than pure science alone, the consultants were armed with immense funds of experience, skill, instinct and decisive judgement as they battled against disease and death. Hospitals then were undoubtedly run by the consultants and for the consultants.

In 1954, the transition from this world to the science-based health service, more exact but less personal, and infinitely more complex and expensive, was just getting under way. Roger himself would eventually join the ranks of the consultants in his chosen sphere of neurology, in which he became a recognised authority. It was this intellectual distinction that led to his appointment as Master of Pembroke College, Oxford, as well as his public renown as a sporting hero. He would sum up the evolution of the National Health Service by recalling that at the beginning it was expected that it would so transform the health of the nation that its cost would soon begin to diminish. This view of course completely failed to foresee the medical advances and inventions, the tide of discovery and innovation in diagnostics, drugs and surgery, that would increase exponentially the demands on every aspect of medicine. The costs and the complexity of the health service prompted politicians to seek ways of rationalising and controlling it, often in ways that were highly confusing and unwelcome to those who worked in it. The result was frequent conflict, minor or major, in the running of hospitals, so that Roger's tact and patience were in great demand for policy planning and daily administration. Against this background Roger worked consistently to care for his patients, but also to keep alive his research ambitions. He realised that no one man could become omniscient in medicine, and that specialisation was the way forward, both for him and for those who would need expert attention. At an early stage he had identified neurology as a potentially vast and exciting field for future research; this came about when still a student at Oxford and he was introduced to Ludwig Guttmann and his work with spinal injuries at Stoke Mandeville Hospital.

But neurology itself was a vast field with many sub-divisions, so that any aspiring specialist would need to mark out a narrower territory to explore and master, and his choice fell upon the autonomic nervous system. This studies those parts of the brain and nervous system which control function not under our conscious control; this ranges from the beating of the heart to reflex actions, such as snatching away one's hand from a flame or hot iron, before the pain has even registered. It is also responsible for innervating the body in moments of risk or danger, the so-called "fight or flight" system, and this particularly interested Roger since it plays a large part in sports. An athlete under stress, say in the last lap of a middle-distance race, can resist tiredness and pain and go into overdrive without the conscious direction of thought, as Roger knew very well from his own experience. He would succeed in his chosen speciality to such effect that he was asked to edit the standard textbook of neurology, written originally by the aptly-named Russell Brain (later Lord Brain) and which was soon doubled in size to 800 pages and became Brain and Bannister's *Clinical Neurology*. This was followed by a more specialised work written with a St Mary's colleague, Chris Matthias, entitled *Autonomic Failure: A Textbook of the Disorders of the Autonomic Nervous System*. One of the well-known disorders of the autonomous nervous system is Parkinson's disease, and it is deeply ironic that, much later in life Roger himself would fall victim to that condition. Typically he made light of it and continued to live a full and normal life for many years after the diagnosis. Late in his life he was asked which of the many awards which he had received was the most important to him, and he named a lifetime's achievement award from the American Academy of Neurology. "This," he said, "is about my life as a whole, and in medicine, which are more important to me than whatever I did as a runner up to the age of twenty-five."

The decision to commit himself to neurology came in 1974 when his life was disrupted, and might have been ended, by a serious car crash, in which he and Moyra were badly injured. Roger came off the worst with a shattered right ankle, which never fully healed, and impaired his walking, although not to a critical degree. If the speed or the angle of the crash had been slightly different they might both have died. The driver of the other car was drunk, and after he himself had recovered, he was fined £25. One of the saddest aspects of this crash was that it marked the final end of his running, which now became quite impossible. Roger considered that he had survived four near-death experiences: the first was in Bath in 1942, during an air raid when a German bomb scored a direct hit on his house, when fortunately he was in an underground air-raid shelter; several hundred other inhabitants of Bath were not so lucky. The second was a climb of the Finsteraarhorn, Switzerland's third highest mountain, with Chris Brasher, who had a daredevil streak, and lured Roger on to this challenge, which was far beyond his limited climbing experience. The season was wrong, they had no local guide, and they were in constant danger of falling into crevaces; there is a fine photograph of Roger on the summit, but he knew that he had taken a foolish risk, and was lucky to get down safely. The third was a narrow escape from drowning when swimming on the Moroccan coast, and he had to swim for his life to avoid being swept out to sea; and the fourth was that car crash. He might have added a fifth, for in the 1970s he took up sailing on the south coast, which he enjoyed enormously, but again he over-reached himself on a long trip. Towards its end, he found himself in the Channel with darkness coming on, tacking in an adverse wind, and with some uncertainty about his exact position. During this ten-hour sail he sensed that he was reaching the absolute limit of his sailing endurance, and, as on the mountain, it could easily have ended in disaster. Another sport which claimed his attention in the 1970s was orienteering, introduced from Scandinavia by fellow-runners Chris Brasher, Gordon Pirie and John Disley. This was safer by far than sailing, although finding oneself lost in woodlands with the night coming on was not unknown.

It was after the car crash, during a recovery period of enforced inactivity, that Roger determined to devote himself almost entirely to neurological research and publishing, although he had long ago identified neurology as his deepest interest: in 1962 he had obtained a travelling scholarship which enabled him to spend a year at Harvard, and with visits elsewhere. He always recalled this as a time of desperate tension over the Cuban missile crisis, rather than any great research achievements. Yet he must have made an impression in America, for two years later he was quite unexpectedly offered the chair in neurology at Albany College in New York state. He was tempted of course by the prospects that this offered, but he declined, characteristically citing his roots and his friends in England, explaining that he owed his ten years of medical education to England, and felt morally compelled to serve England in return; in effect, he was saying that "England made me," but in his case for something far nobler than that which emerges from the Graham Greene novel of that name.

Chapter Eleven: THE OLYMPIC PROBLEM

The Russian mystic, Gurdjieff, once wrote a book called *Meetings with Remarkable Men.* Roger's life too was profoundly affected by the example of a number of remarkable men who contributed to the formation of his intellect and his character. As an influence on Roger's life, his father was clearly in a category of his own, but many others came later, most of them closely associated with Oxford. First there were the runners, beginning with Arnold Strode-Jackson, who won the 1500 metres gold medal in the Stockholm Olympics of 1912; Philip Noel-Baker, silver medallist in the 1920 Olympic Games in Antwerp, and founder of the Achilles Club; and Jack Lovelock, gold medallist in the Berlin Games of 1936. Roger did not of course know these men during their running careers, but he learned about them later, and their presence hovered over Oxford athletics like guiding spirits; they embodied the ideals which Roger adopted and built into his personal philosophy of running. More approachable in human terms was Sydney Wooderson, the diminutive bank-clerk, whose career was interrupted by the war, but not before he had set a new world mile record, a man who did all his training after work, a pure amateur who asked nothing from his sport but the joy of running well. Wooderson came back after the war and scored his greatest international triumph in 1946 when he won gold in the European 5,000 metres championship. He also had the strange experience of setting his world record of 4 minutes 6 seconds for the mile, then some years later running a much faster 4 minute 4 second mile, when that time was no longer fast enough to be a record.

In the medical field, the first inspirational figure was Ludwig Guttmann, the German refugee who was responsible for a revolution in the treatment of severe spinal injuries and the disablement that followed them. Given charge during the war of the small Stoke Mandeville hospital at Aylesbury, he badgered the Ministry of Health unmercifully to get the funding and equipment that he wanted, and within a few years patients who would have died a few months after their injuries would now leave hospital in a wheelchair after six months, with the hope of a new life. It was Guttmann who conceived the possibility of sport for disabled people, and in 1948 he held the first Paralympic Games at Stoke Mandeville; they grew steadily in size and scope and became an integral part of the Olympic Games, summer and winter. In person a forceful, difficult man, very different from Roger, Guttmann nevertheless demonstrated how much a doctor could achieve when compassion, knowledge and determination were linked together.

Among the runners, it was Noel-Baker who went on most clearly to put his ideals into practice in society at large. He was a Quaker and a pacifist, and served as an MP and Labour government minister from the 1930s to the 1960s. After the war he became one of the leading campaigners for nuclear disarmament, being awarded the Nobel Peace Prize in 1959 for his efforts for international peace. Alongside all this political activity he remained deeply involved with sport. He was a senior figure in the organisation of the London Olympics of 1948, and he went on to found the International Council for Sport and Physical Education, the first multinational forum for research and development in sport; when Noel-Baker stepped down as President, Roger succeeded him. Noel-Baker's belief in the therapeutic power of sport in the life of individuals and of nations was unshakeable: he told Roger, "International sport is fast becoming my chief hope for the salvation of mankind".

This was in the 1970s, when clouds seemed to be gathering over the world of international sport in general and over the Olympic Games in particular. The Games seemed to be becoming targets or publicity platforms for various political protest movements, sometimes with tragic results, as in Mexico and Munich. They were also, scarcely less visibly, pawns in the Cold War between the Russian Empire and the West, leading to the boycotts of the Games in 1980 and 1984. Roger was very much opposed to the politicians using sports and sportsmen as pawns in their international chess games. Moreover, the televised Games had become global spectacles, with budgets then approaching a billion pounds, while the movement towards the professionalisation of many Olympic sports was clearly unstoppable. These effects could be seen in the Eastern bloc teams, who were sponsored by the state to win prestige for their countries' socialist regimes, but also in the American university sports scholarships, which were simply another route to that same goal. For the true amateur, who trained only in his spare time, the likelihood of even reaching Olympic finals medals was becoming more and more remote, much less winning medals. In this intensely competitive system, drug-use became an ever-increasing problem, suspected at the time, and finally proved twenty years later when the East German State archives were opened, revealing officially-planned drug programmes used by their sports teams, who had consequently won scores of Olympic medals over the years. The architect of this programme was Manfred Ewalt, who was eventually tried for causing actual bodily harm to hundreds of athletes, some of whom were permanently affected by the drugs; Ewalt was convicted and given a suspended prison sentence.

As these problems became more and more evident, many people took the view that the Olympics had drifted out of control: they were too big, too expensive, too politicised, too much like a form of show-business, while the original principles were being corrupted or forgotten; they also argued that sport was actually harming international relations. When Roger raised these matters with him, Noel-Baker refused to be deflected from his ideals and remained determinedly optimistic, even through the boycott years (the last one he did not witness, having died in 1982). For him, it was the personal camaraderie between the individual athletes that could break down national barriers. Roger was less optimistic, and was especially concerned about the commercial dimension, suspecting that the Olympic hierarchy was unwilling to confront these problems because of the immense sums of money that were on offer when allocating the Games and selling television rights; the temptations to bribery and corruption were just too great.

Much as he admired Noel-Baker, Roger became pessimistic, and in the spring of 2008 he published a major article in **The Times** warning that radical thinking would be needed to save the Games. He reviewed the negative aspects of the Games which were now glaringly obvious, and urged a reduction in their sheer size, suggesting a return to core sports of strength rather than skill; he thought that sports which hold their own world championships every year might not need to be represented at the Games; he thought that a permanent site in Greece could avoid the massive recurring expenditure on new facilities; he looked back fondly to the London Games of 1948, for which no new facilities were built, and the cost was a total incredible by today's standards of £750,000; even the supposedly traditional torch relay came under his critical eye as an unnecessary expense, an argument which he backed up by reminding people that it was first used only in 1936 at the so-called Nazi Games. Most important of all perhaps, he urged that the fight against drug use must be pursued to the utmost, for it was this issue that was sapping the credibility, one might almost say the soul, of the Games.

One issue that he did not address in this particular article, although he wrote about it elsewhere, was the flag-waving nationalism that is so dominant: should this really be central to sport? Why must we long for "our" athletes to win, to humble the rest of the world, to demonstrate our superiority? Can we not admire and applaud the best man, irrespective of his nationality? Noel-Baker was probably right that to athletes themselves, the personal camaraderie was important, but to the thousands watching in the stadium and the millions watching on television, the patriotic emotion was more so. To the news media in every country, national fervour was para-

mount in selling their broadcasts and their newspapers. These feelings had been growing in Roger's mind for a long time, and a number of documents exist which makes
this very clear. A long speech given in 1979 in his capacity as President of the
I.C.S.P.E, he had rehearsed all these same arguments: the drugs, the politics, the
nationalism, the professionalism, size and cost of the Games in an age that was supposed to have discovered that small is beautiful, and the suggestions for reducing their
scale – all these were brought forward as evidence for his case. In 1992 he wrote:

> *This is Olympic year and it is time to take stock of modern sport, its problems
> and its potential. The British government has just contributed £55 million to a poten-
> tial £1 billion for the next Olympic Games in Manchester, yet elite sport has become
> ever-more driven by commercial forces, and is plagued by an increasing number of
> injuries... Corruption and dishonesty in sport, including shameful drug abuse, need
> ever-more complex administrative and legal controls to restrain them. We seem to live
> more in the age of the "professional foul" than in that of "fair play". Yet there is still a
> desire to see high sporting achievement, to see athletes struggling to get the best out
> of themselves in a world that is increasingly mechanical and regulated.*

This was a bleak assessment, possibly written with Ben Johnson's drug-taking
disgrace at Seoul still fresh in the mind. Manchester of course did not host the
Olympics, and sixteen years later, with the London Olympics just appearing on the
horizon, he was writing in a similar vein. What then was Roger's verdict four years
after the *Times* article, and having witnessed the 2012 Games? Were his earlier
doubts and foreboding justified? The answer is no, they were not: on the contrary,
they were swept away in a tide of euphoria, which followed from the highest number
of medals ever won by a British team. The athletics were superb, whether won by
British sportsmen or not, and he welcomed this success as a massive source of inspiration for the next generation. The drug control programme had taken thousands of
samples, and no high-profile drug scandals had marred the Games. There were no
serious political tensions. He felt confident that the legacy from the Games, in the
form of the superb Olympic Park, would be a key to future performances in many
sports. The cost, at £9.4 billion pounds, appeared almost reasonable compared with
Beijing's $40 billion in 2008, and the atmosphere of the Games had been excellent,
after the oppressive state control seen in China. Roger was evidently delighted with

all of these outcomes, and said that he felt the golden age of his youth, in athletic terms, had never gone away. There is no doubt whatever that this response to the Games was heartfelt and genuine, and that it reflected the majority view throughout Britain; however there are certain qualifications which must be made.

The first is that some eight years after the Games evidence emerged that they had not been drug-free after all. A re-testing of stored samples revealed scores of adverse findings, leading to results being overturned and medals being cancelled. The number was not huge, but neither was it insignificant, and in athletics one in seven medal-winners were retrospectively stripped of their prizes. Weightlifting, dominated by Russia, fared much worse with 40% of medals being cancelled, and a senior Russian coach confirmed that their teams had used widespread doping. No British or American athletes were downgraded in this re-testing exercise. Second, it emerged from a number of social studies of the physical legacy in the Olympic Park, that the Games has yielded only meagre gains for local people. Much land had been used for building flats priced far beyond their reach, and the same is true of many of the facilities and cultural centres. Neither of these matters has any connection with Roger, and his death in 2018 spared him the distress that he would have felt had he known about them.

But there are other areas which are relevant to Roger's thinking, and they are the money and the state's role in sport. Back in the days of the Sports Council the mission statement, the motto, was "Sport For All", and this was the ideal which Roger continued to promote all his life. So we have to ask what could the Sports Council have done with £9.4 billion pounds? How many permanent facilities, how many sports parks, spread democratically around the country, could have been built for that sum? In those days too, Roger often discussed the question of state help for certain chosen athletes, to enable them to compete more evenly at the elite level, and in those days he was opposed to it as incipient professionalisation, or as he put it, "paying athletes to become temporary civil servants". In fact in the mid-1990s Roger did offer his endorsement of a plan for sports scholarships to be operated through the universities, but this scheme was overtaken by the appearance on the scene of the National Lottery and its funds. Roger had envisaged spending £10 million pounds on 2,000 scholarships of £5000 each, but the system that was adopted was administered by Sport England (the renamed Sports Council) working through the governing bodies of the individual sports.

In the 2012 Olympics, the record number of British medals of all grades was known to be the direct result of this state-sanctioned support, whose aim was to buy glory for Britain, which was exactly what nobody had wanted in the past. For a long time we had condemned the state funding of national sports teams, especially from the Eastern bloc, but now we had apparently learned the old lesson that if you can't beat them you have to join them. So, having said that intense nationalistic feeling at the Olympics was probably a bad thing, there must be a sense of unease at the idea of giving direct state funding of athletes, however that funding is structured; for how else can it be interpreted except as a desire to win national prestige? Moreover, after reaching an elite level of performance, and gaining fame in the Olympics, athletes could take part in the Diamond League series of events, which features all the biggest stars of the day, a system analogous to the long-established professional tennis circuit, which made its stars into millionaires. In this new environment, success at the Olympics would open the way to a professional athletic career with very high financial rewards, and of course ever-higher demands in terms of training. Professional sport was looking more and more like a branch of show-business, and by the 1980s athletics had certainly become a television sport. One striking symbol of this is the wild displays of emotion that winning athletes indulged in after crossing the line; shouting, jumping, punching the air, rolling on the ground – all this became normal, working up the drama for the global television audience.

Yet it seems that Roger too had to accept that sport changes as the society around it changes. The golden days of his youth had not returned, and they never would; he had to retain it in memory alone. His vision of the pure amateur, running solely for the joy of running and of self-discovery was still valid for the enthusiastic amateur; but such an amateur could forget the Olympic Games, the European Championships or the Commonwealth Games, for there was now an unbridgeable gulf between himself and those magnificent displays of speed and strength. The ambitious athlete must give his entire life to his sport, and therefore he must tap into the funds which would enable him to do that. This is professionalism, and one of the problems with professionalism, its money and its star-system, is that it makes other levels of sport appear unimportant, not worth discussing, which is the reverse of the truth. The private discipline, the personal journey of self-discovery, the friendships with other like-minded enthusiasts – these are the truly therapeutic aspect of sport, not the glamour, the stardom and the wealth of the millionaire. The modern worship of success cannot and should not reach into the private world of the amateur athletes, for they are now the ones who keeps alive the Olympic ideal: that it is the endeavour, the taking part, that is vitally important. We need to remind ourselves frequently that athletics is not synonymous with the Olympics, just as the Tour de France is not synonymous with cycling. Both those events have long been at the storm-centre of conflict and controversy, seized on and whipped up by the media for all they are worth.

Meanwhile ordinary athletes and cyclists whom no one has heard of and who do not appear on television, have been training and racing for their own reasons – for excitement, achievement, self-fulfilment and wellbeing, and these are the individuals who stand at the real heart of sport. Part of Roger's own resistance to the hard-work school of extreme training was that it meant sacrificing all other aspects of life, which he had emphatically no desire to do. He wanted his medical career, family life, social life and outside interests of many kinds. He did not want to become a running machine, for that would be a sacrifice too great to pay for success. When he learned of Jim Ryun's intense training regime in the 1960s, which took him to a four-minute mile at the age of seventeen and to a world record at twenty, he was frankly shocked, regarding this regime as life-destroying rather than life-enhancing. Ryun's later misfortunes perhaps lend some credibility to this view. From Roger's writings and speeches and from his conversation, a definite sense emerges of a struggle in his mind between wishing to pay tribute to the athletes of the day, while feeling privately saddened by the passing of the amateur spirit of the past, and regretting the star culture of professional athletics. Roger's contribution to this debate about the nature of sport in modern society, its huge potential value and the temptations towards the betrayal of its traditional ideals, justify his status as a leading philosopher of sport, a status that was of course hugely strengthened by his own example and career achievements.

Chapter Twelve: PEMBROKE AND AFTER

In the mid 1980s, while holding on to his core activity in neurological research in St Mary's and the National Hospital, Roger began to shed some of his medical work. The reason for this was his appointment in 1984 to the position of Master of Pembroke College, the terms of the appointment allowing him still to spend a number of days each week in London. Mastership of a college had become a highly visible role in leadership within the Oxford community, and in interaction with the larger world outside. A Master needed wide skills in diplomacy and negotiation, and a grasp of detail. In his social and quasi-political work over twenty-five years, Roger had clearly shown his ability to work around difficulties and to get things done. A college Master should also be a figurehead commanding respect, and one could hardly think of more popular and respected figure than Roger, in Oxford and throughout England too. Maintaining the academic reputation of the college and its physical fabric were both paramount if students and staff were to be attracted, and to this end fund-raising was at or near the top of the agenda, and here again no figure better known or more highly regarded could be found to negotiate on the college's behalf than Roger. Whichever way they looked at it, the college seemed to have chosen a winner.

On his side, his loyalty to Oxford was absolute, as was his belief that Oxford had given him almost everything of value in his adult life; consequently he was filled with a deep desire to give something back. He had of course already given Oxford his own unique legend as an athlete, but his post-athletic career had armed him with the power to give something more, something hard, tangible and practical, for example, to direct an entire college, which was truly a challenge that he could relish. Pembroke wanted to expand, and needed to do so to compete for students with the larger and more famous colleges; it needed to acquire a higher profile and a clearer identity. The classic way for almost any institution to achieve this is to build, and in plain terms, Roger's brief was to raise the millions of pounds needed to erect a new, up-to-date students' centre, for their accommodation, study and social life. To this end he set out to tap into the unknown thousands of Pembroke alumni around the world, to enlist their enthusiasm and their money to burnish the image and the reputation of the college. Roger identified a number of potential cells of Pembrokians who were prepared to work for the good of the college; there might be a doctors' cell, a lawyers cell, a business and industrial cell, a London cell and an American cell, all united in affiliation to the ideal of reviving the college. The success of this approach was revealed five years after Roger's appointment, when the new student building beside the river, upstream of Folly Bridge, was opened. Castle-like in design, it consisted of one hundred rooms, two quadrangles, and the necessary meeting and leisure rooms.

On a rather different level, Roger was taken aback to learn that the last time that Pembroke rowers had gone head of the river was in 1872. Surely, he thought, that could be improved upon, and to do so would boost the morale of all those involved in the life of the college. Again, Roger took up the cause, and with the financial support of several generous alumni, new boats were acquired and professional coaching was found. The results were more than satisfactory, since the Pembroke male rowers went head of the river in 1995, two years after Roger's retirement. Perhaps this demonstration of professional planning in sport contributed to Roger's acceptance of that principle in the Olympic sports generally. On her side, Moyra thoroughly enjoyed her occupation of the Master's lodgings. She had never stopped painting and sketching, and one of her hobbies was to take a sketch-pad to the many occasions, formal or informal, which she attended with Roger, and to sketch the speakers, the guests or the musicians; the result was a lively artistic record of those academic and social gatherings.

Each May since 1954 had seen some form of celebration of the anniversary of the four-minute mile, indeed as time passed the celebrations seem to have been more visible rather than less. No doubt this was because it offered an opportunity for a nostalgic look back to the 1950s; many people have stated that they could remember the day of hearing or seeing the news of the four-minute mile, just as they did the day of the assassination of President Kennedy. The year 1994 witnessed a unique gathering in Oxford of all the world mile record-holders from 1954 to that date: Bannister, Landy, Ibbotson, Elliott, Snell, Jazy, Ryun, Bayi, Walker, Coe, Cram, and Morceli; from before the four-minute mile, Andersson and Wooderson were also present. The only absentee was Ovett, who by that date had become, shall we say, an idiosyncratic character, and had made many statements to the effect that breaking athletic records, and indeed athletics itself, were both a waste of time. The others would all disagree, indeed they were very conscious that their world mile records had given them a unique place in the history of the sport, as no other distance could do, and that part of that mystique was due to Roger's senior role as a figurehead. The photographs taken at that reunion can be added to the marvellously evocative images which already existed from the golden years of Roger's career, whether the classic solitary figure, almost airborne, leaping across the line at Iffley Road, or those that captured every moment of the tense struggle with Landy. A documentary film was also released and televised: entitled "Chasing the Dream", it was extremely well researched, showing original film of all the athletes in their record races and face-to-face interviews with them; it remains a unique document in the history of athletics.

The four-minute mile was a memory which, by popular request it seemed, was never allowed to die. In 2004, the fiftieth anniversary saw events honouring Roger in Oxford and elsewhere, ranging from having his image stamped on the 50 pence coin, to the Coop brewery producing a "Golden Mile" ale. It is a pity that no one thought of renaming the Iffley Road track in Roger's honour for these celebrations, but it came three years later. The press was filled with recollections of him and tributes to him, and the flow of fan mail which had begun in May 1954 reached new heights. One of the most delightful fan-letters he ever received belongs to this year, but relates more closely to his birthday in March, and it came in the form of a poem from a woman who proudly claimed kinship with him, writing from Colne in Lancashire:

> *Kind greetings Sir Roger for March twenty-third,*
> *"Happy Birthday to You", the song which is heard.*
> *We know much about you from TV and Press,*
> *Your splendid achievements can't fail to impress.*
>
> *Your countless successes in "Who's Who" appear,*
> *An athlete superb, a fine doctor's career.*
> *Your four-minute mile, supreme triumph and fame,*
> *A unique event bringing world-wide acclaim.*
>
> *It's fifty years now since that May the sixth date,*
> *A remarkable milestone which you'll celebrate.*
> *Although you don't know us, we're of the same clan.*
> *A Bannister lass our great grandmother Ann.*

Roger Bannister   Athlete and Philosopher

She wed Thomas Chadwick, their daughter was Jane,
At Trawden Jane dwellt, Job Lane Farm in Job Lane;
She's our great grandma, Thomas Bracewell she wed,
From Trawden our forebears, we're Colne born and bred.

Apart from one month, you and I the same age,
Best wishes we send with these lines on this page.
From Renée and Stuart to you here's a toast:
Please send a signed photo to us in the post!

Renée Patricia Blackburn, 20 March 2004.

I love this poem, and we can well imagine how it would have delighted Roger, who had spent some time reading up on his family's Lancashire roots, mainly thanks to an uncle who had gone very thoroughly into the matter and left careful records. The poem seems to sum up the way so many people felt about Roger. Without ever having met him, he was a figure in a kind of national pantheon, whom they could admire and relate to; below royalty of course, but far above politicians and above most show-business names, but perhaps on a level with treasured actors and actresses such as Alec Guinness, David Niven, Valerie Hobson and Deborah Kerr, all best seen in black and white, like Roger. A second piece of memorable fan-mail came from a fellow doctor, evidently with a mathematical brain, who wrote, without a covering letter:

1 mile = *15 mph*
  = *360 miles per day*
  = *131,400 miles per year*
  = *6,570,000 miles per half century*

You could have girdled the earth 304 times by now:
That's some circumnavigation!
Congratulations!

Decennial celebrations of the four-minute mile had become more or less obligatory, but those of 2014 might well have been overshadowed by the public announcement that Roger had been diagnosed with Parkinson's disease. However, he had no intention of letting that happen; on the contrary, he was buoyed up by the launch of his new book, *Twin Tracks*, which continued the autobiographical narrative begun sixty years before in *First Four Minutes*. The purpose of the book was clearly to show the way in which his life's motivation, his ideals about athletics and its relevance to life, had not disappeared when he stopped running, and nor had his desire to succeed and to excel. These things remained constant, but he had found new ways to express them, to embody them in social action channelled into medicine, the politics of sport, and education.

Twin Tracks had an unusual background in a writing project which occupied him during 2000-2001. This project represented an ambitious return to writing, for it gave a fuller and more personal account of his early life than that which had appeared in *First Four Minutes,* and it then went on to chart the course of his life after 1954. When he began work on the new book, he had four children and innumerable grandchildren, who were growing up in a world utterly different from the world of his own youth. He therefore conceived the idea of addressing his "Life Story Part Two" to his extended family, and he gave it the title *Letters to my Grandchildren*, although they were not literally sent as letters. He wanted to leave the new generation of Bannisters with an honest picture of life as it had been in England over the previous sixty years, and a clear account of their family origins. This book was not commercially published; instead a small number of copies were privately printed in 2001 for circulation among the family. It was so well received that Roger was urged to publish it in the normal way, but he hesitated, still viewing it as a private memoir. However he had become motivated about writing again, and during 2007-8 he enrolled in a creative writing class in the Continuing Education department of Oxford University. He wrote a dissertation on "The Origins of the First World War", was highly commended, and received his diploma.

This pleased him enormously and it also weakened his resistance to publishing the *Letters* volume; probably his health situation played a part too. Eventually, after considerable re-writing and more urging from his family, he decided that the sixtieth anniversary of the four-minute mile in 2014 would be a suitable moment to bring out the book, and to show that the two sides of his life were linked by strong ethical ideals, which, as no one could help noticing, were under pressure, perhaps even struggling for their survival. He made this life statement deliberately late, after his retirement from Pembroke College, when he was no longer burdened by his responsibilities to institutions and committees in which he had been involved for almost his entire life. *Twin Tracks* has a corresponding feeling of tranquillity, in which he recalls gratefully his life in a free and civilised country among friends and family, and his final hope was for the continuity of this way of life. If anyone in our time had ever helped to contribute to that civilisation and that continuity, it was Roger Bannister, who died in Oxford on 3 March 2018.

Postscript: THE LEGACY

At the end of December 1999, on the very eve of the millennium, a magnificent luncheon banquet was given at the Mansion House in London, its keynote being "A Celebration of Success." It was previewed as "The Lunch of the Century" in the press, which then took great delight in reporting the innumerable broken hearts among the nation's elite subjects when they realised they had not been invited. Nevertheless, in the presence of Queen Elizabeth and the Duke of Edinburgh, five hundred guests were called together for a glittering afternoon of self-congratulation. The great and the good of every kind were there: artists, scientists, politicians, academics and scholars, actors and actresses, churchmen, military top brass, captains of industry, financiers, and those in every category of distinction imaginable. Only one man there was unclassifiable: he might have been called an icon or a history-maker, but no label was necessary, because he was simply Roger Bannister. He was *the* man of the 1950s, the man who excelled all the others at that luncheon – except of course the Queen – in fame, affection and public respect; the man who had created a legend of physical heroism, and had then shown that he had a precious and more universal example to show us: that of a fully integrated personality, a thinker, a philosopher and a man of action, leading an ethical life. The demands on him during the years since 1954 had been enormous, and merely being Roger Bannister was a full-time career. It goes without saying that no one else could possibly have done it, but still we wonder how he stayed calm and sane with so many individuals, groups and institutions seeking his attention.

Among all that gathering of people, he was possibly the least possessed of direct power or great wealth, but he had found something better in his life, and curiously enough the organisers of the banquet had found an admirable motto from Confucius to print on the programme, and which applied perfectly to him: "What the superior man seeks is already in him; what the common man seeks is in others." Roger had spent his early life seeking what was already in him, namely the power to become the most brilliant runner of his generation. But when he reached that peak, he ceased running; he descended from the summit and re-entered normal life as a humanist, seeking to do what he could to heal people's bodies, and heal the society in which they lived. His legacy is not the bricks and mortar of new college buildings in Oxford, nor the grand dinners with the elite of society, although he was a gregarious man, and he was himself an excellent speech maker. When he stood up he already had the respect of his listeners, and when he sat down he had truly added something new to their lives through his clarity of thought and his modesty of manner.

The interesting thing about Roger as a star is that the elite, the great and the good, were attracted to him, *they* sought *him* out, not the other way around. They recognised his innate superiority and his ethical integrity, a man who had achieved a unique physical mastery over himself, and who spoke with the special authority of an athletic hero, but also that of the philosopher. If they had read his books, or even *First Four Minutes* alone, they would have received the impression of a young man who was drawn forward by a sense of his own destiny. He read mountaineering books, such as Herzog's *Annapurna*, the story of the first ascent of an eight-thousand metre Himalayan peak, and he was enthralled by the sense of conquest, of going where no human being had ever gone before, and the sacrifice and anguish that attended such a great feat. His personal theory of harbouring nervous energy in order to release it in the big race was his own discovery and his own creed, formulated in his childhood. This was his unique weapon which brought him so many victories, and it suggests that he was a man who might have done anything that he put his mind to. He could certainly have become a writer; as a politician he would have been an excellent M.P., but surely would not have got far up the greasy pole of power. As a man of warm humanity and a keen ethical sense he might have chosen the Church as his spiritual home, but its doctrines and dogmas did not appeal to his rational sense. Medicine was his ideal: scientifically precise but infinitely variable, it satisfied his intellect, his imagination and his faith in positive action to make the world, in however small a way, a better place. But to the young, his message was simpler: it was the virtue of physical endeavour, of tenacity and endurance, in forming a unity between mind and body. If this is formed in one's youth it becomes a possession that will serve us all our lives. "What sport does," he wrote, "is to return us to the lost world of nature, to the intense excitement of the primitive vigilance in which our survival or success depends on our speed, strength and agility." Running in particular is a solitary activity, in which thought, logical, conceptual thought, is dissolved in the sense of physical wellbeing, even when taken to the level of pain and struggle. The mind is virtually switched off, and we are left only with a sense of purpose, as the body feels only a consciousness of the air, the wind and the earth beneath us. We are set free from civilised idleness and boredom, and we re-create our life-sense.

To this cultivation of a private philosophy of sport, Roger brought his innate sensitivity and honesty, and he was a great link with the past, when beliefs and ideals gave meaning and value to life, not wealth and material possessions, success and stardom. He exemplified Newman's belief that "No great work is ever done by a system, whereas new systems arise out of the individual." His views on sport were always those of a purist who looked back with affection and wistful regret to the old-fashioned amateur ideal. He recognised that he must move with the times, but he did not relish the media-circus culture that had overwhelmed the Olympics Games. He took considerable pleasure in the 2012 London Games, to which he was invited as an elder statesman and a guest of honour, because it passed off without scandals or disasters of the kind that had marred so many previous Games. He had no desire to criticise or belittle the athletes of the modern day, but still he saw himself as a custodian of the ideals of the past in an age of relentless change and innovation. If questioned about the Games, he would continue to suggest quietly that they might perhaps be a little too big, too triumphalist and too expensive, and in need of a fresh approach. In 2015, just one year after *Twin Tracks* was published, his family had privately printed an album of copies of his own published journalism from 1951 to 2012, an invaluable collection and a strong reminder that he could, had he wished, made a career as a writer

Roger has been dead for six years now, so that he belongs to history; but he is thought of with immense respect and affection by many, many people. When I think of him, he has no age, he is old enough to be calm and wise, and young enough to be an athlete speeding around the track or training in the open countryside. The best evocation of him that I can think of is the poem which he admired so much and quoted in *First Four Minutes,* surely one of the few poems ever written about running. I see the reading and enjoyment of this poem as summing up his message to us, and as a small but important part of his legacy.

Song of the Ungirt Runners

We swing ungirded hips
And lightened are our eyes,
The rain is on our lips,
We do not run for prize.
We know not whom to trust
Nor whitherward we fare,
But we run because we must
Through the great wide air.

The waters of the seas
Are troubled as by storm.
The tempest strips the trees
And does not leave them warm.
Does the tearing tempest pause?
Do the tree-tops ask it why?
So we run without a cause
'Neath the big bare sky.

The rain is on our lips,
We do not run for prize.
But the storm the water whips
And the wave howls to the skies.
The winds arise and strike it
And scatter it like sand,
And we run because we like it
Through the broad bright land.

- Charles Hamilton Sorley, 1895-1915

APPENDIX

The Track Is Yours
The Times   14 August 1955

This was Roger's first article published under contract to "The Times" following his retirement from running. From 1951 onwards he had occasionally published reports of athletic events as "Our Special Correspondent" without his name appearing. For this he was obliged to obtain the permission of the Amateur Athletic Association, as he did also for a proposed book on sports physiology, although in the end that was never written.

The Englishman plays games with a fervour which he seldom seems to devote to real life. Other countries may compliment us on our constitutional system, or our invention of trade unions, but they reserve their deepest awe for our devotion to sport. The happy British knack of adapting and popularising games has spread more widely than the sterling area. Hockey, soccer and Rugby football were all invented in England. The Swiss never climbed mountains until an Englishman asked the way to the summit. Skiing to the Scandinavians was a means of transport until, with rare perspicacity, an Englishman showed that it could be developed as a sport to the financial advantage of countries with snow and mountains. The world still gasps at the originality of our most exasperating invention – cricket – and does not know what to make of it. Perhaps foreigners see in it only "a game for two played by twenty-two."

Since the war, the standard of British athletics has soared. After the first post-war Olympics at Wembley in 1948, the tide of popularity for this sport, although increasing throughout the world, has been most spontaneous, most irrepressible, in Britain. Its only rival in the international sphere seems to be soccer. Athletics in Britain has became a dramatic, crowd-riveting sport. More than 100,000 athletes keep in regular daily training, sacrificing other pleasure to running faster, jumping higher or throwing further than their fellows. Many of them run more than ten miles a day, the equivalent of four times round Hyde Park (including vaulting the fence into Kensington Gardens), or forty times round the Oval. Emerging from this turmoil are the few exceptional but unimportant champions. Like meteors, they run their course until they burn themselves out, breaking records in the process. But the champions are not the real athletes. In a single race, over 1000 of Britain's cross-country runners struggle through mud, rain and barbed-wire entanglements for the national cross-country championship. Every July, 2000 selected track athletes wrestle for national, junior and senior titles.

Athletics is no longer the sport of students and Servicemen. Our schoolboys are nurtured by 1400 qualified, honorary coaches, who in their spare time pass on the knowledge they have learned from national coaches at Loughborough and other summer schools. Spectators share in the general enthusiasm, some showering on athletes the plaudits they had previously reserved for greyhound racing. They are also learning to be critical, hitherto the preserve of the Scandinavians. A British crowd recently showed by slow hand-clapping its disapproval of a mile race that failed to develop at the expected speed. But there is one man who is genuinely puzzled by this athletic revival. The armchair televiewer takes a long sip of his iced orange as he watched yet another British athlete, overtaken by fatigue and heat, collapse into the outstretched arms of his coach. He is mystified by the sight of so much apparently useless physical effort, but he cannot take his eyes from the screen. He is a new factor in the sport. He asks why we do it. As performers, perhaps we owe him an explanation.

Why do we play any game? Perhaps we enjoy struggling to get the best out of ourselves, whether we play games of skill requiring quickness of eye and deftness of touch, or games of effort and endurance like athletics. It is not just the desire to succeed. Hacking a golf ball from the rough satisfies as powerful an instinct as sinking a smooth putt on the green. We run not because we think it is doing us good but because we like it and cannot help ourselves. We enjoy the companionship of others engaged in like efforts. The track freindships I made were forged by the tension and excitement of races. This "baptism under fire" gives them a strange permanence. But there may be deeper reasons that we hardly dare to admit to ourselves; a reason that lies locked away in the more primitive part of our souls. Thoreau once commented, "The majority of men lead lives of quiet desperation". We may strap-hang morning and evening to reach our polished world of desktop size, or we may tighten 1000 identical nuts daily on some part of Britain's new car, but do we not still seek instinctively some of the freedom that our far-off ancestor knew when he chased sabre-toothed tigers across Salisbury Plain?

The need for adventure was at first satisfied by the struggle for survival. Having however now conquered so many of the natural dangers facing him, man demands further trials. Unless he finds them, may he not rebel with shocking violence or depravity? Is it not possible that the drift towards crime may be the thwarting of simpler pleasures? "Breathes there a man with soul so dead" that he had lost the urge to impress on the world the indelible mark of his personality? In sport, a man finds a trial for life more active than a game of chess, more exciting than digging the garden. We have used machines to conquer land, sea and air. Athletes realise that if this quest for speed is worthwhile it is better to choose the running track. There we can still feel that out bodies have a skill and energy of their own, apart from the man made machines with which we spend our working week. There, we can fight a pitched battle against the claustrophobia of out time. The new Don Quixote can tilt a vaulter's 15-foot pole at the crazy windmill of modern life, or defiantly hurl a 16-pound shot.

I believe that some of the restlessness of an industrial age that in other countries has caused revolutionary eruptions has in Britain safely extinguished itself in the games we play. But as the drag of passive leisure increases, we need a fiercer sport like athletics which shakes our roots more deeply with confusing pattern of success and failure. Athletics provides an outlet for the craving for freedom, an outlet which will become more important the more restricted, artificial and mechanised our society and work become. It has many advantages. You can do it in your own time, whether you are on day or night shift. You can choose your own event among the many which suit different physiques, the long and thin, the broad and strong. Unlike most ball games, natural aptitude is less important for it than industry and perseverance. Except in terms of energy and effort, it costs no more than a pair of running shoes. No one can say "You must not run faster than this, or jump higher than that." The track is yours, there is no limit.

Photographic Section

1. Family Background and Childhood   86

2. Oxford - the Early Years   92

3. St Mary's and the Helsinki Olympics   100

4. Vindication - Running into History   104

5. Vancouver and Bern   120

6. Athletes of the Bannister Era   138

7. Marriage and Family   144

8. Elder Statesman of Sport   156
    and Master of Pembroke

The contents of these pictures are not covered by the Index

Section One

Family Background and Childhood

Above: the Victorian family, c.1896. Roger's paternal grandparents with their eleven children. The youngster in the centre is Roger's father, Ralph.
Below: Park Hill, Barrowford, home to the Bannister family from the 1500s to the 1700s, and now a local heritage centre.

The 1890s in Lancashire: not much evidence of running prowess in the family yet, but the uncles were clearly keen cyclists. The lower picture shows the takeover around 1890 of the safety bicycle from the fearsome penny-farthing above. Some fifteen years after these pictures were taken, Ralph Bannister, Roger's father, would take up running, and win his school mile championship.

Left, Roger's parents, Ralph and Alice, aound 1930.

*Below,
also around 1930,
Alice with Joyce, age three,
and Roger around eighteen
months.*

Right
Joyce with puppy
Roger with train.

Below,
Joyce age eight,
Roger age six.

Above, parents and children 1954, the annus mirabilis.

Below, evacuated to Bath at the age of ten, Roger went on to win the junior school cross-country championship three times in succession. This picture appeared in the Bath press.

Two views of Bath.

Right, part of the almost endless stepped path up to Beechen Cliff, which Roger climbed and descended every day to and from school, the first training challenge of his life. Below, the view from the top.

Section Two:

Oxford - the Early Years

Above, leading in his first mile race and his first race at Oxford, the Freshmen's Sports, 1946. Result, second place to T. Curry, no 26.

Below, Exeter College Athletics Club, 1948.
Roger seated, second from right.

Below, a chilly-looking start to the Oxford v. Cambridge cross-country meeting in 1949, Roger looking downcast.

In his diary, Roger described the thrilling sprint finish to this race with Daniel Gilbert (see above p.15). In 2004 he was delighted to receive this letter and photograph from his Cambridge rival.

Roger Bannister   Athlete and Philosopher

Looking surprisingly youthful, Roger trains here on Harrow School cricket ground, date unknown, but presumably while staying with his parents during a vacation.

A venerable bearded professor of Cologne University greets an Oxford athletic team during a goodwill visit to Germany in 1947. Roger was in the team but not visible here; instead Norris McWhirter is featured

Above, March 1947, Roger has just won the Oxford v. Cambridge mile at the White City, and talks to Harold Abrahams at the reception afterwards; Roger in convivial mood, and he recalled this meeting as a blissful haze, when he also met Jack Lovelock.

Below, the 1949 Oxbridge v. the American Ivy League Universities; Brasher behind Roger and to the right.

Roger Bannister   Athlete and Philosopher

*Two photographs
at Iffley Road.
Top event unknown.*

*Lower picture Roger
appears to be
demonstrating his
airborne galloping
technique.*

*Right: Victory in the 1951
Benjamin Franklin Mile, a
very prestigious event in
Philadelphia, entry by
invitation only.*

*Below: the chief interest of
this picture is the massive
margin by which Roger was
capable of winning some of
his races; British Games,
White City, 1953.*

In America for the 1949 Ivy League matches, Roger met his great hero Jack Lovelock, then living and working as a doctor in New York. Lovelock died at the very end of that year.

1951, and his Oxford career is approaching its close.

Preparing for a cross-country event, or perhaps just a training session.

Summer 1950, graduation day, his first medical degree.

Section Three:
St Mary's and the Helsinki Olympics

Victory in the 1951 AAA Mile Championship at the White City.

*Amateur athlete and amateur actor: Roger appearing in Wilde's
"Lady Windermere's Fan", with St Mary's Dramatic Society .
How did he find the time ?*

Victory in the inter-hospital cross-country, 1952.

Below:
Receiving the AAA half-mile Championship trophy from the Queen and Princess Margaret. The Queen asked Roger was it not more usual for him to run the mile? Perhaps she had even read in the press about the controversy surrounding his training in this Olympic year.

*Left: Olympic training
at Harrow in the
spring sunshine.*

*Below:
The 1500 metre final,
first lap, Roger exactly
in mid-field.*

Above:
The final bend, eighty
metres to go. Lueg leads
from Barthel, Macmillen,
Roger and El Mabrouk.
Barthel and McMillen
would pass Lueg, Roger
kept his place and was
fourth, with El Mabrouk
fifth.

Right: Roger waiting on
the track for his heat, close
to Landy; at this point they
had not met.

We do not normally think of Roger as a relay runner but in 1954 he was a member of a team which set a new 4 X 1500 metres world record. These two superb pictures capture the last baton change with Brian Hewson handing over to Roger, and the finish of the final leg. A wet day at the White City brings out the pain and commitment of middle-distance running.

How fortuitous that he wears the number A1 !
He gave no account of this race in his book "First Four Minutes", but he had
been involved in another relay the previous year, see page 120.

Section Four:

Vindication - Running into History

Above:
Training with Chris
Brasher at Paddington
track through 1953 and
spring 1954.

Right:
A snapshot taken a few
weeks before the four-
minute mile.

Above: the start of the mile, Iffley Road track, 6 May 1954

Below: the first lap, Brasher, Bannister, Chataway.

The half-way mark, Brasher still leading, but Chataway will soon move into the lead; the effort is plain to see.

The finish, the time 3:59.4.
Probably the most famous photograph in athletic history.

*An alternative view of Roger breaking the tape, looking back
along the home straight to where Chataway is speeding towards
second place, 7 seconds behind his history-making friend.
It has been said that some 2000 spectators watched the race, but
without this picture you would not guess it.*

Yet another unfamiliar view of the finish looking across the track centre; the BBC camera is raised up left of centre.

Images of exhaustion, confusion and disbelief, but not yet joy.

By now they know the time, and that sporting history has been made.
The long-term effect on their lives they could not yet guess.

The athletes and the coach, Franz Stampfl. Roger did not have a formal relationship with Stampfl, as the two Chrises did, but he paid a full tribute to the encouragement that Stampfl gave him. The coach's reputation was of course enormously enhanced by his involvement in the four-minute mile.

*Some three hours after the Oxford mile Roger has been rushed down to
the BBC in London to appear live on Sportsnight and be interviewed by Peter
Dimmock. Relaxed and debonair, Roger's new life was about to begin.*

A very comical picture of Roger the morning after the four-minute mile.
emerging from his parents's house in Harrow to find that he was being
"doorstepped" by pressmen and neighbours.

*Greeted on the morning of 7 May by the junior doctors and
students at St Mary's Hospital.*

Meetings with royalty were to become almost routine.

White City August 1953, a new 4 X 1 Mile World Record, set by (left to right) Chataway, Seaman, Bannister and Nankeville. The total time was 16:42.8, Roger's individual time was 4:7.6. I am not sure if this record is still actively competed for. Each runner ran alone, not against a rival team member, so it was four solo time-trials. Nankeville was three time national mile champion before Roger became dominant,

A convincing victory in the 1954 AAA mile championship, only weeks before his historic race against Landy in Vancouver.

Section Five:

Vancouver and Bern

*The race between Bannister and Landy at the British Empire
Games in Vancouver in August 1954 attracted enormous pre-race
publicity. They were the only two four-minute milers in the world,
and the race was christened the Mile of the Century;
it did not disappoint.*

The start: Landy is in the inside lane, ready to move into the lead at the earlist possible moment; Bannister is in mid-field. No one expected anything other than a two-man race.

Down the home straight for the first time. Landy's pace was too fast for everyone else, including Roger, who allowed a significant gap to open rather than try to stay with Landy stride for stride.

By the end of the second lap Landy's lead looked enormous - over ten yards - and Roger was receiving no pacing help, he was was completely detached from his rival. He realised that he must start to pull Landy back: he could not permit him to draw any further away, nor could he leave everything to the final lap. From this point on Roger quickened his pace, while trying to harbour as much precious strength as possible .

*This splendid shot was taken at the moment the bell sounded for the last lap.
It shows that Roger had completely closed that fearful gap, and that everything was down to which man had the greater reserves. Had Roger exhausted
himself prematurely, and was Landy still running within himself?*

*One of the most famous moments in athletic history. On the last bend, a few
yards befor entering the home straight, Roger launches himself past his rival;
but at that exact moment Landy glances over his left shoulder in a desperate
attempt to see if Roger is behind him or not.*

*Probably a single second after the previous picture, Landy turns his head to
see Roger striding away with no more than seventy yards to the finish line.
Both men are at their limit, but Roger has gained a few vital yards and Landy
will not catch him; the margin of victory was five or six yards.*

*The bizarre sight of an English team official dashing onto the track
to catch Roger as he collapses at the tape; in the background Landy's
face seems to show no emotion.*

Back on his feet

The podium: Roger's time was 3:58.8, Landy's 3:59.6. Landy's world record had survived, and the four-minute barrier had been broken by two men in the one race. Ferguson of Canada was third in 4:4.6

Roger with Jim Peters, the English runner who collapsed with total exhaustion at the end of the marathon, not long after the climax of the mile race. Roger visited him later in hospital. At this time Peters held the world record for the marathon.

Roger with his gold medal. The Vancouver mile is widely regarded as one of the most thrilling races ever seen, between the two greatest milers of their generation.

*The over life-size bronze statue of Bannister and Landy
that was erected in 1964 in the Vancouver stadium.*

Bannister and Landy:
image and reality thirty years later.

The European Athletics Championships, Bern, August 1954, the early stages.

Entering the back straight in the last lap: the strain is telling but Roger looks perfectly positioned and in control. Some twenty seconds later he will seize the lead and hold it to the finish.

Bern: Two different angles on the last strides of the last race of Roger Bannister's running career, both pictures demonstrating his airborne technique.

This time he did not collapse at the tape.

Section Six:

Athletes of the Bannister Era

Two figures who were inspirational for Roger: left, Jack Lovelock, the New Zealander who studied at Oxford and won gold at the Berlin Olympics; and right Sydney Wooderson, Britain's leading pre-war miler.

Below: the star of the 1948 London Olympics, Fanny Blankers-Koen of Holland (right) winner of four gold medals, here very narrowly beating Britain's Maureen Gardner.

*Chris Chataway's cele-
brated victory over
Vladimir Kuts, when
he took Kuts's world
5000 metre record.
Run during a floodlit
evening event at the
White City in October
1954, it was watched
by millions on
television.*

*Left, Derek Ibbotson beats Chataway in a desperate
sprint finish for the AAA 3-mile title in 1956.
Below: Arthur Wint, Olympic 400 metre champion, the
first of the great Caribbean sprinters.*

Left, Gordon Pirie struggles valiantly against the Russian iron man Vladimir Kuts at the Melbourne Olympics.

Right, Chris Brasher's greatest moment, taking the steeplechase gold medal at Melbourne in 1956.

Late in his career the great Zatopek leads Pirie, Ibbotson and Chataway.

Left, the immortal Zatopek on his way to victory in the Helsinki Olympic marathon, having already won the 5000 and 10,000 metre crowns.

Herb Elliott who shattered the world mile record at the age of 20. Two years later he won the Olympic 1500 metres Gold in Rome, also breaking the world record. Elliott had an air of invicibility that unnerved Roger.

143

Roger Bannister   Athlete and Philosopher

In 1955 Brasher persuaded Roger to try some serious Alpine climbing, their target the Finsteraarhorn, the third highest peak in Switzerland.

Below: they succeeded in their goal, but something in this photograph suggests that the strain was fairly severe.

Above, the summit, Brasher at the top, Roger scrambling up.

Below, evidently the Alps held other attractions than snow and rock. On the left is John Tyson, an athlete and climber who took most of the pictures.

Section Seven:

Marriage and Family

Two portraits, informal and formal.
The wedding took place in Switzerland where
Moyra's parents lived.

An unusual guard of honour was provided by a group of local athletes.

Back in London to receive the CBE for the four-minute mile.
Only two guests are permitted, so Roger's father nobly stayed at home.

DECEMBER 30 1954

THE LISTENER

1141

The Queen's Christmas Day Broadcast

Her Majesty's message to the Commonwealth

IT is two years since my husband and I spent Christmas with our children. And as we do so today, we look back upon a Christmas spent last year in Auckland, in hot sunshine, 13,000 miles away. Though this was strange for us, we felt at home there, for we were among people who are my own people and whose affectionate greeting I shall remember all my life long. They surrounded us with kindness and friendship, as did all my people throughout the mighty sweep of our world-encircling journey.

Nevertheless, to all of us there is nothing quite like the family gathering in familiar surroundings, centred on the children whose festival this truly is, in the traditional atmosphere of love and happiness that springs from the enjoyment of simple well-tried things. When it is night, and wind and rain beat upon the window, the family is most conscious of the warmth and peacefulness that surround the pleasant fireside. So our Commonwealth hearth becomes more precious than ever before by the contrast between its homely security and the storm which sometimes seems to be brewing outside, in the darkness of uncertainty and doubt that envelops the whole world.

active world many people are leading uneventful, lonely lives. To them, dreariness, not disaster, is the enemy. They seldom realise that on their steadfastness, on their ability to withstand the fatigue of dull, repetitive work, and on their courage in meeting constant small adversities, depend in great measure the happiness and prosperity of the community as a whole.

When we look at the landscape of our life on this earth there is in the minds of all of us a tendency to admire the peaks and to ignore the foothills and the fertile plain from which they spring. We praise—

A new photograph of the Queen with her two children
Marcus Adams

and rightly—the heroes whose resource and courage shine so brilliantly in moments of crisis. We forget sometimes behind the wearers of the Victoria or George Cross there stand ranks of unknown, unnamed men and women, willing and able if the call came to render valiant service. We are amazed by the spectacular discoveries in scientific knowledge, which should bring comfort and leisure to millions. We do not always reflect that these things also have rested to some extent on the faithful toil and devotion to duty of the great bulk of ordinary citizens. The upward course of a nation's history is due, in the long run, to the soundness of heart of its average men and women.

And so it is that this Christmas Day I want to send a special message of encouragement and good cheer to those of you whose lot is cast in dull and unenvied surroundings, to those whose names will never be household words, but to whose work and loyalty we owe so much. May you be proud to remember—as I am myself—how much depends on you, and that even when your life seems most monotonous, what you do is always of real value and importance to your fellow men.

I have referred to Christmas as the

not only a time for family reunions, for paper decorations, for roast turkey and plum pudding. It has, before all, its origin in the homage we pay to a very special Family, who lived long ago in a very ordinary home, in a very unimportant village in the uplands of a small Roman province. Life in such a place might have been uneventful. But the Light, kindled in Bethlehem and then streaming from the cottage window in Nazareth, has illumined the world for 2,000 years. It is in the glow of that bright beam that I wish you all a blessed Christmas and a happy New Year.

Racing with Time

BY ROGER BANNISTER

I SHOULD like to give my views about some problems we all face. They are only my own views, and I am sorry only a one-way traffic is possible—a joint discussion would be so much better. Although I cannot speak for anyone else, I can say that the background that helped to form my views is common to many other young people. It is not a background that gives any special knowledge of politics, foreign affairs, or economics, and I have had little time to follow newspapers closely or any other sources that influence or mould opinion.

What is this background that I share with so many other young people? We were born to uncertainty in the nineteen-thirties. In vulnerable areas we were brought up with a violent shock when the exciting prospect of war to a ten-year-old turned into the bewildering succession of air-raid warnings, evacuation, and broken schooling. After the war crisis followed crisis. The arms and machinery of wars, including atomic

weapons, were being amassed and there was always the danger that one side might pull the trigger in panic. This country seemed at times like a still, small voice trying to take an independent line, but without any means of persuading the two potential combatants to listen to her. In addition to all this outward confusion there was also the confusion of faith and ideas. Within the communist world the existence of God was denied and membership of a church was almost an offence in itself; what would happen when a whole generation of young people had grown up without full knowledge of Christianity or any non-marxist faith? We wondered, was the only defence against this creed the creation of another equal and opposite dogma? If in America a youthful indiscretion of a shilling subscription to the Communist Party could jeopardise a man's subsequent career, was there really very much to choose between the two sides?

The feeling of impotence to affect the course of affairs increased if

Roger, given the freedom of the press to analyse the world's ills, shared the page with the Queen, see page 1 of the Prologue.

Roger, the two Chrises and Gordon Pirie were enlisted to publicise a charity for the restoration of London churches; Prime Minister Churchill gives them his blessing.

Below, Moyra the artist in her London studio, before the calls of family life took first place.

Moyra Bannister's Sketch Books

Moyra led a very busy social life, expecially once her four children had grown up, and when Roger became Master of Pembroke College. One of her chief pleasures was to take her sketch book to social occasions and set down images of who and what she saw, often adding her off-the-cuff comments.

Roger bearing up manfully under the weight of family duties. The two on the top of the heap are certainly enjoying themselves, but the one at the bottom looks to be in pain.

In any collection of old pictures you will find some puzzles, some oddities and some downright mysteries, and this is one of them. It clearly shows Roger, smartly dressed and apparently darting across a traffic-filled road in an American city. What can he be doing, and who took the photograph ? The only rationalisation that I can offer is that it may not be quite what it seems: he is not risking his life, because the traffic is not moving - it is waiting to move on when a light changes or something similar. This idea is supported by the fact that the wheel of the big truck is clearly not revolving. We know that Roger was in America three times between 1949 and 1954, but it seems highly unlikely that we shall ever know the story behind this bizarre picture.

Back in America about thirty years later for another mystery: Roger fires the start gun for a celebrity race. Famous names include Peter Snell, Filbert Bayi, Steve Cram and Jim Ryun, but place and date unknown.

Section Eight:
Elder Statesman of Sport
and Master of Pembroke

The Sports Council was initially founded in 1965 by the Labour government under Harold Wilson. It was an advisory body which reported and made recommendations to a new Ministry of Sport, whose job was to finance and improve sport in Britain. Five years later under a new government, it was re-founded as an independent agency with executive powers and its own finances. Having been on the council from the beginning, Roger was asked to serve as overall chairman in the new phase. He spent altogether nine years bringing into being hundreds of sports facilities throughout Britain, under the slogan "Sport for All ". The Council was later re-branded as Sport England.

*Roger's role involved travelling around the country, often acccompanied
by Moyra, opening sports centres of all kinds. His immense prestige
contributed greatly to the success of the entire scheme, and it was for
his work for the Sports Council that he received his knighthood in 1975.*

When he was asked which of the many awards that he had received meant the most to him, Roger would point to this award from the American Academy of Neurology. This, he said, was a tribute to the work of his lifetime in medical science, not any particular success that he had achieved.

With Lord Stockton (Sir Harold Macmillan) one of the hundreds of distinguished guests welcomed by Roger to Pembroke College.

The Master of Pembroke College, 1984 -1992,
the official portrait by Peter Greenham.

A distinctly unofficial portrait with a couple of close friends,
the Chrises Brasher and Chataway.

Roger attended almost every Olympic Games from 1956 to 2012.
Here he holds the torch at Athens in 2004.

Elder statesman of British and world athletics.

In May 1994 a unique gathering took place in London of 14 holders of the World Mile Record. Seen here in chronological order are: Wooderson and Andersson (pre-four minutes), Bannister, Landy, Ibbotson, Elliott, Snell, Jazy, Ryun, Bayi, Walker, Coe, Cram and Morcelli. Ovett did not attend. The reunion was organised by Steve Cram.

Two highly influential figures in Roger's life and thought: above, Ludwig Guttmann of Stoke Mandeville, pioneer of paraplegic medicine and sport.

Below Philip Noel-Baker, Olympic medallist in 1920, politician and govern-ment minister, peace campaigner, Nobel prize-winner, and President of the International Council for Sport and Physical Education, a forum for the pro-motion of peace through sport. Roger succeeded him as President.

*Good humour and camaraderie between two runners, after
supreme triumph for one and deepest disappointment for the
other; Roger with Landy after the Vancouver mile.*

In 1949 a young man looks thoughtfully towards the future,
which now appears to us a heroic and distant past,
which we must try to hold on to.

Sources

The Roger Bannister archive in the Bodleian Library Oxford contains extensive original documentation and pictures, general collection number is 11527. Direct quotations from this collection are listed below by file number. The photographs in this book have been provided by the Bannister family.

p. 16 Exeter College Prize, 11527/29

p. 16 Plan to reform the University Athletic Club, 11527/ 31

p. 17 Diary from the 1940s, 11527/3

p. 39 Philosophy class story, 11527/32

p. 40 John Landy letter, 11527/31

p. 43 Mal Whitfield story, 11527/32

p. 51 On marathon running, 11527/23

p. 53 Testimonials as a young doctor 11527/29

p. 59 "Sport", from the BMC Journal 23/12/1972, 11527/55

p. 60 Sievert Prize speech, 11527/29

p. 67 Philip Noel-Baker, 11257/55

p. 69 Olympic reflections, 11257/55

p. 75 Bannister family poem, 11257/35

p. 76 Circumnavigation letter, 11257/35

p. 77 Creative writing diploma, 11257/29

p. 79 Lunch of the Century, 11527/29

p. 80 "The lost world of nature", Sunday Times, 6 July 1958

Bibliography

Roger Bannister: **First Four Minutes**, 1955; autobiography, the fundamental source. New expanded edition, 2004.

Roger Bannister: **Twin Tracks**, 2014; autobiography, mainly after the running years.

Frantisek Kozik: **Zatopek the Marathon Victor**; biography, 1954

The Achilles Club: **Athletics**, 1955; authoritative survey of the sport in the 1950s.

Derek Ibbotson: **Four-Minute Smiler**; autobiography, 1960.

Herb Elliott: **The Golden Mile**; autobiography, 1961.

Brian Hewson: **Flying Feet**; autobiography, 1963.

Gordon Pirie: **Running Wild**; autobiography 1961.

Graeme Woodfield: **Jack Lovelock: Athlete and Doctor**; biography, 2007.

Arthur Lydiard: **Run to the Top**; revolutionary distance coaching, 1967.

INDEX

Abrahams, Harold, 15, 25, 51

Achilles Club, 50-51

Aden, National Service in, 54

Alexander, Field-Marshal

Amateur Athletic Association, 58

Andersson, Arne, 15

Bannister, Alice (née Duckworth, mother) 11

Bannister, Moyra, née Jacobsson (wife) 50, 55-56

Bannister, Ralph (father), 10

Barthel, José, 26, 27, 30, 43, 44

Bath, Bannister family evacuated to, 11

Benjamin Franklin Mile, 24

Bingham, Bill, 21

Blankers-Koen, Fanny, 18

Boxing, Bannister criticises, 59

Brain, Russell, 63

Brasher, Chris, 30 ff

Breckenridge, Alec, 43

British Empire Games, Vancouver, 1954, 40 ff

Cerutty, Percy, 33

Chariots of Fire, film, 15

Chataway, Chris, 26, 30, 31 ff

Compton, Dennis, 9

Confucius, 79

Coubertin, Pierre de, 20

Cross-Country Running, 17

Curry, T.P.E., 17

Diamond League Athletics, 71

Doctor in the House, film, 1954, 62

Duke of Edinburgh Award Scheme, 53

Elliott, Herb, 46

Erikssen, Henry, 19

European Athletics Championships, Bern, 1954, 43-44

Everest, first ascent, 9

Ewalt, Manfred, 67

Exeter College, Oxford, 14, 15, 16 ff

First Four Minutes, book, 45

Four-Minute Mile Reunion, 1994, 74

Gardner, Maureen, 19

Gehrman, Don, 24

Gerscler, Woldemar, 30, 48

Gilbert, Daniel, 17

Griffiths, Eldon, 58

Gurdjieff, George Ivanovich, 65

Guttmann, Ludwig, 63, 66

Hägg, Gunner, 9. 34

Hahn, Kurt, 54

Harris, Reg, 9

Harrow, 10, 26

Harvard Scholarship, 1962, 65

Herzog, Maurice, *Annapurna,* 79

Hewson, Brian, 46

Howell, Dennis, 57

Hunt, Sir John, 54

Ibbotson, Derek, 46

Iffley Road Track, 14, 16, 31, 34 ff

International Council for Sport and Physical Education, 67

Journalist, Bannister as, 50-52

Kuts, Vladimir, 33

Lancashire, Bannister family origins, 10-11, 75-76

Landy, John, 31, 33, 34, 38 ff

The Listener, 7

Letters to My Grandchildren, book, 77

Lovelock, Jack, 15, 21, 22

Lowe, Douglas, 47

Lunch of the Century, 1999, 78

Lydiard, Arthur, 49

Macmillan, Don, 32

Manley, Dorothy, 19

Matthews, Stanley, 9

McWhirter twins, Ross and Norris, 33, 34, 35

Moran, Charles (Lord), 25

Moss, Stirling, 9

Motspur Park Track, 32

Mountaineering, 22, 30, 64

Nankeville, Bill, 19, 26

National Association of Boys' Clubs, 51

National Hospital, Bloomsbury, 62

Near-death experiences, 64

Neurophysiology, 17, 63

New Zealand Centennial Games, 22

Newman, Cardinal J.H., 80

Newton, Isaac, 62

Noel-Baker, Philip, 66

Nurmi, Paavo, 38

Olympic Games and Cold War, 67

Olympic Games, Paris, 1924, 15

Olympic Games, Berlin, 1936, 15

Olympic Games, change and controversy, 65 ff

Olympic Games, London, 1948, 18 ff

Olympic Games, London, 2012, 69, 70, 80

Olympic Games, Melbourne, 1956, 42, 56

Olympic Games, Mexico, 1968, 52, 68

Olympic Games, Munich, 1972, 60

Olympic Games, Helsinki 1952, 9, 22, 25 ff

Olympic Ideal, 20, 29, 40, 66 ff

Orienteering, 65

Orwell, George, 54

Oxbridge School of Athletics, 47 ff

Oxbridge v. Ivy League Universities in U.S.A., 20

Oxford University Athletic Club, 16

Paddington track, 31, 34

Paralympics, 66

Pembroke College, Oxford, 63, 73-74

Philosophy of Sport, 59, 67-72, 80

Pirie, Gordon, 46, 48 ff

Plowden Committee on Primary Education, 55

Prospect, book, 54-55

Published Articles by Sir Roger Bannister, 80

Queen Elizabeth II, 7, 78

Respiration physiology18, 22-23

Richards, Tom, 19

Ryun, Jim, 72

Sailing, 65

Santee, Wes, 32

Sherrington, Sir Charles, 17

Sievert Prize, 60

Snell, Peter, 46

Sorely, Charles Hamilton, 45
Sport For All, motto, 58
Sports Council, 56
St Mary's Hospital, Paddington, 25, 30
Stacey, Nick, 26
Stampfl, Frantz, 33, 35, 58
Strode-Jackson, Arnold, 66
The Track Is Yours, Appendix, 82
Training, schools and theories, 23, 31
University College School, 13
White City Stadium, 15
Whitfield, Malvin, 43
Williamson, Audrey, 19
Wilson, Harold, 57
Wilt, Fred, 24
Wolfenden Report on sports funding, 57
Wooderson, Sydney, 15, 16
Zatopek, Emil, 18, 23, 26, 28, 33